The Great Grace

The Great Grace

Receiving Vatican II Today

Edited by Nigel Zimmermann

LONDON · NEW YORK · OXFORD · NEW DELHI · SYDNEY

T&T CLARK
Bloomsbury Publishing Plc
50 Bedford Square, London, WC1B 3DP, UK
1385 Broadway, New York, NY 10018, USA

BLOOMSBURY, T&T CLARK and the T&T Clark logo are
trademarks of Bloomsbury Publishing Plc

First published in Great Britain 2015
Paperback edition first published 2019

Copyright © Nigel Zimmermann, 2015

Nigel Zimmermann has asserted his right under the Copyright, Designs
and Patents Act, 1988, to be identified as Author of this work.

A catalogue record for this book is available from the British Library.

ISBN: HB: 978-0-567-65731-2
PB: 978-0-567-68685-5
ePDF: 978-0-567-65732-9
ePub: 978-0-567-65733-6

A catalog record for this book is available from the Library of Congress.

Typeset by Deanta Global Publishing Services, Chennai, India

To find out more about our authors and books visit
www.bloomsbury.com and sign up for our newsletters.

Contents

Acknowledgements

This project represents the combined efforts of a number of hard-working folk in Sydney, Australia and international contributors.

The chapters themselves are the refined versions of seven plenary addresses given at *The Great Grace: Receiving Vatican II*, hosted by the Archdiocese of Sydney in May 2013 to mark the *Year of Grace*, an initiative of the Australian Catholic Bishops Conference. We are grateful for the time and energy put into the addresses which were outcomes of quality scholarship and examples of clear thinking with and for the Church.

Heartfelt thanks are given to the following people whose hard work and commitment made this an extraordinarily successful event: Emma McDonald, Katrina Lee, Selina Hasham, Kristina Vasiliadis, Jake Ryan, James van Schie, as well as Chaline Taylor and Ian Steigrad of Epic Conferences and Events.

Although the conference was hosted to celebrate the *Year of Grace* in the local context of the Church in Sydney, it became a welcoming event for guests from around the world and a point of focus for many in Australia, with over 600 registered attendees including an extraordinary number of Catholic teachers. This special year, from Pentecost 2012 to Pentecost 2013, was intended as an opportunity for Australian Catholics to take up the challenges in St John Paul II's apostolic letter addressed to the Church at the close of the millennial year, 2000, *Novo Millennio Ineunte*, as they relate to the mission of the Church. Especially pertinent for the bishops were two phrases of the late pontiff: to 'contemplate the face of Christ' and 'starting afresh from Christ'. Soon after the Australian bishops decided in favour of this initiative, Pope Benedict XVI announced a *Year of Faith* for the universal Church to celebrate fifty years since the opening of the Second Vatican Council. The Australian Church recognized this as a gift and chose to view both 'years' in tandem with one another, and local dioceses were asked to initiate ways of celebrating each of these as appropriate.

As a major event in Sydney, the conference enjoyed the generous sponsorship of the Australian Catholic University and the Catholic Education Office, each of whom recognized the conference as a formative opportunity in the life of the Australian Church. In addition, the following organizations lent significant support through financial and practical means: Catholic Cemeteries and Crematoria, archdiocesan Liturgy Office, Australian Catholic Superannuation and Retirement Fund, Corrs Chambers Westgarth, Avium Projects, Invocare, Telstra, University of Notre Dame Australia, Ord Minnett, Makinson d'Apice Lawyers, Moore Stephens, Fuji Xerox and Ray's Florist, as well as volunteers from Campion College and the Catholic universities who helped to look after the many attendees.

As an archdiocesan event, special gratitude is expressed to the (then) Archbishop of Sydney, Cardinal George Pell for being a gracious host and participant, and to (then) Auxiliary Bishop of Sydney, Most Rev. Peter Comensoli, who took up the task of leading the organizing committee.

To complement the plenary addresses were a series of workshops given by specialists across Australia in various topics, including conciliar humanism, the Church's mission, indigenous peoples and Vatican II, evangelization, Catholic Social Teaching, liturgical art and architecture, the new ecclesial communities, the vision of Pope John XXIII, power and authority in the Church, women and the Council, marriage and family, interreligious dialogue, youth ministry, lay leadership, ecumenism, moral teaching and communicating in the online and digital age. The vision of this conference was broad and deep and we are thankful for the rich contribution of workshop presenters.

Appreciation is offered to the publisher, T&T Clark Bloomsbury, for the dedication given to this project. Special mention should be made of two plenary speakers whose pastoral commitments prevented them from publishing their work in this collection, Most Rev. Arthur Roche, Secretary of the Congregation for Divine Worship and the Discipline of the Sacraments, and Most Rev. Allen Vigneron, Archbishop of Detroit. Each travelled a significant distance to share pastoral and theological wisdom with conference attendees.

In addition, it is important to remember another plenary speaker, Most Rev. Michael Putney, Emeritus Bishop of Townsville, who had kindly taken up the invitation to speak at the conference but sadly passed away in the preceding months.

All those who gave generously of time and resources for the conference are acknowledged with sincere gratitude. It is hoped the present collection will foster a wise and deliberate commitment to the Council in the years ahead.

List of Contributors

Dr Nigel Zimmermann
Institute for Ethics and Society, University of Notre Dame Australia

George Cardinal Pell
Prefect of the Secretariat for the Economy

Marc Cardinal Ouellet PSS
Prefect of the Congregation for Bishops

Professor Anne Hunt
Executive Dean of the Faculty of Theology, Australian Catholic University

Professor Tracey Rowland
Dean, Pontifical John Paul II Institute for Marriage and Family, Melbourne

Rev. Professor Anthony Kelly CSsR
Professor of Theology, Australian Catholic University

Dr Austen Ivereigh and Mr Jack Valero
Catholic Voices UK

Most Rev. Mark Coleridge
Archbishop of Brisbane

Most Rev. Peter A Comensoli
Bishop of Broken Bay

Documents of the Second Vatican Council

Constitutions

Dei Verbum	18 November 1965	*DV*
Lumen Gentium	21 November 1964	*LG*
Sacrosanctum Concilium	4 December 1963	*SC*
Gaudium et spes	7 December 1965	*GS*

Declarations

Gravissimum Educationis	28 October 1965	*GE*
Nostra Aetate	28 October 1965	*NA*
Dignitatis Humanae	7 December 1965	*DH*

Decrees

Ad Gentes	7 December 1965	*AG*
Presbyterorum Ordinis	7 December 1965	*PO*
Apostolicam Actuositatem	18 November 1965	*AA*
Optatam Totius	28 October 1965	*OT*
Perfectae Caritatis	28 October 1965	*PC*
Christus Dominus	28 October 1965	*CD*
Unitatis Redintegratio	21 November 1964	*UR*
Orientalium Ecclesiarum	21 November 1964	*OE*
Inter Mirifica	4 December 1963	*IM*

Introduction

Nigel Zimmermann

For three days in 2013 (20–23 May), over 600 people gathered in Sydney to attend an international conference titled *The Great Grace: Receiving Vatican II Today*, hosted by the Archdiocese of Sydney. The proposal to host an international conference of high calibre was taken during the pontificate of Benedict XVI. However, as providence would have it, the actual event was to take place three months after the unexpected election of Jorge Bergoglio, the first South American and first Jesuit Bishop of Rome. Pope Francis has captured the world's attention with gestures of compassion for the poor, the sick and the suffering, and has preached the Gospel with attention to the simplicity of following Jesus Christ. Francis, building on the extraordinary theological achievements of his predecessors, embarked immediately upon a programme of reform in the Catholic Church, including significant structural and financial changes in the Vatican. Indeed, the (then) Archbishop of Sydney, Cardinal George Pell, whose chapter opens the present collection, was, in the first half of 2014, called to Rome to become prefect of a new body associated with these changes, the secretariat for the economy. Calls for a transparent, efficient, regularly audited set of financial structures in Rome have been heard by the Holy Father not merely for the sake of avoiding scandal, but for the purposes of fulfilling the Christian mission without unethical and unnecessary bureaucratic hindrance.

However, in his provocative call for a 'poor church that is for the poor', and in his various interventions in interviews, face-to-face encounters and his preaching, Francis, named for the great reformer St Francis of Assisi (1181/82–1226), has issued calls for a much deeper reform than the offices of Vatican bureaucracy. He has invited all Christians to hear the call of the Second Vatican Council to encounter Jesus Christ, and to follow him with total abandon. There is no substantial or doctrinal disagreement between

Francis and the Pope Emeritus, Benedict XVI, nor with John Paul II, the major implementer of the documents and directions bequeathed by the Fathers of Vatican II. However, there is a difference of emphasis in some of his concerns for social and economic questions, and a distinctively new style in the use of popular interviews and off-the-cuff remarks to express the message that Francis wishes to send to his audience. While Benedict XVI and John Paul II had given lengthy, substantial interviews, Francis has pitched his answers to questions posed in shorter interviews in more popular magazines. In this way, the rich theological resources left by the written legacies of Benedict and John Paul are being complemented – perhaps even completed – by the freshness of Francis' approach. For example, witness the warm embrace between his friends Rabbi Abraham Skorka and Omar Abboud at the Western Wall in Jerusalem, or the spontaneous decision to baptize the father of a victim of a ferry disaster in Korea, or Francis' notion of 'proximity' as a core value in his sense of ecclesiology and mission:

> I see clearly that the thing the church needs most today is the ability to heal wounds and to warm the hearts of the faithful; it needs nearness, proximity. I see the church as a field hospital after battle. It is useless to ask a seriously injured person if he has high cholesterol and about the level of his blood sugars! You have to heal his wounds. Then we can talk about everything else. Heal the wounds, heal the wounds … And you have to start from the ground up.[1]

Here, the Church is understood as the nearness of the God of mercy, of a community that is close to those who suffer and ready to attend to the wounded. These words are echoed time and time again by Francis, who is the first pope since the Second Vatican Council not to have been present as a participant. With the election of Bergoglio, the Church is led not by a Father of the Council, but a Son of the Council, a man whose work and ministry has been constantly shaped and formed by the reforms of the Council. Francis did not influence the Council; rather, the Council influenced him. Surely, in Francis, the Church has entered a new era in which the Council may be reflected upon with a balanced historical perspective, and one more attuned to what the Holy Spirit

---

[1] Francis, Pope Francis interviewed by Fr Antonio Spadaro, S. J. (ed.), *La Civiltá Cattolica, America Magazine* (30 September 2013).

has achieved in the intuitions and lessons of the conciliar documents. Indeed, the emphasis upon 'proximity' by Francis profoundly reflects the opening words of *Gaudium et spes*:

> The joys and the hopes, the griefs and the anxieties of the men of this age, especially those who are poor or in any way afflicted, these are the joys and hopes, the griefs and anxieties of the followers of Christ. Indeed, nothing genuinely human fails to raise an echo in their hearts.

With this focus on what is 'genuinely human', the Church, from the Council to Francis, has embarked on a reform process that delves deeply into the sources of its own rich tradition and casts itself as the provocative call to love and solidarity with the human person in the contemporary world. Fifty years on is a happy milestone at which the 'joys and the hopes, the griefs and the anxieties' of the present age can be reflected upon with some maturity. The Council, with a view to both its historical context and to the broader mission of the Church to the poor and afflicted, remains a rallying call for Christians to consider the radical nature of discipleship in Christ and the beauty of faith.

In the following chapters, these lines of thought are expressed with a spirit of joyful theological sobriety. Because the writers of this book attend carefully to the texts of the Council and are persons whose lives and vocations reflect a deep investment in the Church, they are able to avoid the tediousness of short-term agendas and the distraction of short-sighted ecclesiological disputes. Moreover, there is a personal dimension to these texts that adds to the colourful and embodied story of how the Council has unfolded in the lives of so many Catholics.

The opening chapter by Cardinal George Pell is a characteristically direct and intriguing reflection on his experience in the Church in Australia, and on the controversies and challenges that took place. There is both sadness and joy here, especially when His Eminence recalls the many who left the priesthood and religious life in the years that followed the Council. George Pell's episcopal ministry in Australia was often spent defending the Church against public detractors, but on display here is his own academic interest as a historian, and his joyful focus on the role of the Church in the currents of history. This is of great interest given his role as a member of Pope Francis' Council of Cardinal advisors and his office as Prefect of the Secretariat for the Economy. Cardinal

Pell has taken on a significant office of reform as part of Pope Francis' efforts and offers a candid and important reflection here, with one eye on history and the other on the mission of the Church.

The personal and historical recollections of Cardinal Pell, who opened the *Great Grace* conference, are followed by the words of one of the great theologian-cardinals of recent times, Cardinal Marc Ouellet, Prefect of the Congregation for Bishops. Cardinal Ouellet is a Canadian prelate whose works have focused on building up an ecclesiology of *communio*, and his previous works include *The Relevance and Future of the Second Vatican Council* (Ignatius Press, 2013), and *Divine Likeness: Toward a Trinitarian Anthropology of the Family* (Eerdmans, 2006). Ouellet expresses depth and scriptural warrant for his *communio* vision of the Church of the Second Vatican Council, and it is poignant that he couches this as a theology that is still being built and with a view to the future of the Church. Perhaps this is a great work that has only just begun in the Catholic tradition. As Ouellet clearly shows, the texts of the Council direct the Church's ecclesiology towards the hope of reunion, and do so as part of a Christocentric theological tapestry that intersects the Trinity in the life of the human person; thus bearing itself out in a daring Christian anthropology.

It is an exciting development that the Church in Australia boasts world-class lay theologians such as Professors Anne Hunt and Tracey Rowland. Anne Hunt, sometime Executive Dean of the Australian Catholic University (the largest English-speaking Catholic university in the world) provides an important account of the vocation of the laity in the theology of Vatican II. Hunt gathers significant texts on this theme and renders a provocative assessment of possibilities for the future. There is an amplitude of hope here, but also the challenge to continue to reflect deeply and prudently.

Tracey Rowland, Dean of the John Paul II Institute for Marriage and Family (Melbourne) and a member of the International Theological Commission (ITC), places the theological turn of the Council in the context of Australia, emphasizing the move from what she calls correlationism to Trinitarian Christocentrism. Illustrated with concrete examples, Rowland notes a contrast between interpretations of the Council by theologians associated with the *Concilium* journal and *Communio* journal. For Rowland, the theology of Vatican II has a fundamentally Christocentric focus which is framed and built within a rich Trinitarian understanding of God. As such, attempts to correlate aspects of the surrounding culture to touchstones of the Catholic faith are problematic and follow a line of thought that ultimately departs from the vision of John XXIII who opened the Council.

But how might a Vatican II theology be put forward in a culture soaked in modernity, and in which Christianity is often viewed as an oppressive footnote in history? A successful British example is given by Austen Ivereigh and Jack Valero in their work for Catholic Voices. Here, a lay-led initiative came about in response to the visit of Benedict XVI to the United Kingdom in 2010, drawing on the expertise, experience and professional profiles of articulate lay 'voices' in the Catholic world. In the lead up to the pope's visit, when news outlets sought views on various Church-related matters, a ready network of informed lay people were trained and prepared to speak charitably and honestly from a perspective of faith. This avoided the limitations of 'spokespeople' from the Church or the lack of strategic media plans that united dioceses across the nation, and instead gave a very human face to whatever was in the news on a particular day. Much can be said about the theological dimension of what Ivereigh and Valero call 'reframing' and it serves as an eloquent example of the Council's expression of the Church's confident dialogue with its contemporaries in the modern world.

Anthony Kelly CSsR, a celebrated redemptorist theologian who has served as the Australian member of the ITC, invokes the tension between spirit and letter to envisage how the Council might be interpreted. For Kelly, both joy and disappointment followed the Council. Nevertheless, with a poetic sense of the drama of theological truth, Kelly argues for a poignantly human element in interpretation, one that is open to the revelations of history as it unfolds but one that allows the myriad of voices to speak in witness to what is good. He draws comment from sources such as St Therese of Liseux, Jean-Luc Marion, Christoph Theobald, the Council Fathers and Bernard Lonergan (to name a few), and does so with an awareness of how the Council attempted to reach the contemporary human person – man, woman and child – with the light of the Word made flesh, the Christ. In Kelly's reflections, a profuse sense of renewal and adventure is manifest.

Nevertheless, there is constant need to address the significant question as to how Catholic thinkers are to understand the culture in which they do their work. Biblical scholar Mark Coleridge, Archbishop of Brisbane, outlines various terms associated with the 'secular', including secularization, secularity, and secularism. By drawing from the multi-layered biblical tradition of the Church, Archbishop Coleridge argues counter-intuitively that the present cultural context owes more to Christianity than modern secularists realize. He calls for scholars to make critical judgements about what terms they use and what they mean by them, and does so in light of the Council and John Paul II's invitation for us each to allow ourselves to be face-to-face with Christ. In a sign that Coleridge, like others in this book, have taken Vatican II to heart, he suggests that certain language be adopted despite it sounding more evangelical than Catholic, for the faith is to be proposed to all, and not only to those already familiar with Christianity.

Peter Comensoli, Bishop of Broken Bay, offers a concluding reflection that places the previous chapters in light of a biblical image, that of the great stream of goodness as witnessed in the vision of the Prophet Ezekiel. Readers are invited to take part in the pilgrimage which leads to, and is immersed, in that stream, and which the Second Vatican Council articulated with theological and pastoral hope.

This book is a remarkable collection from prelates and laypersons who love the Church and have put their minds to a difficult task: to think with and for the Church. It is the culmination of much work and preparation from the contributors as well as those who worked together so beautifully to host a major influential conference in Australia. It is a sign of the energy and conviction of Catholics in Australia, as well as the fruitfulness of intellectual collaboration between theologians from international and local contexts. Moreover, the array of Catholic school teachers, seminarians, religious brothers and sisters, university lecturers, evangelists, clergy and bishops, media professionals, and enthusiastic sponsors present at the conference was inspiring, and bodes well for the future. Indeed, organizers of the conference will not soon forget that we reached capacity and that bookings had to come to a halt.

The *Great Grace* refers to the grace of the Second Vatican Council as a divine gift, not received as a one-off historical event, but as an unfolding gift in the life of the Church. The fruits of the Council, and indeed of the conference this book comes from, will continue to blossom as provocations of beauty that direct us to higher things. As such, the words gathered here are a testimony to grace and an edification for all those open to beauty, truth and goodness.

Yesterday's Council for Tomorrow's World

George Cardinal Pell

An edited version of a talk given by His Eminence (then Archbishop of Sydney) in St Mary's Cathedral, 20 May 2013, to open the conference, the Great Grace.

Introduction

Most of the younger and middle-aged Catholics in Australia imagine, if they think about it at all, that Church life in their country has been as it is today for longer than anyone cares to remember. Most would concede that their grandparents were better at churchgoing than they are and most cannot remember a big number of religious brothers or sisters teaching in our schools. In one grade six Confirmation class in Melbourne, some years ago, one boy asked me what a nun was! Nearly all my teachers were brothers and nuns.

With this background, it is not surprising that most have little awareness of even the existence of the Second Vatican Council (1962–65) and no idea at all of its importance and the changes it brought to Catholic life in Australia. I am not sure that it is better known than the Council of Trent; rather it is as unacknowledged as the Council of Nicaea.

I should make a couple of points about the title of my reflection. It is difficult enough to discern what is important today in the swirl of news reports and events, before we think about tomorrow. Tomorrow there will be many Catholic 'worlds' across the globe, i.e. different pastoral situations and even in Australia and they will continue to change. Probably the major currents of opinion will be regularly hostile, although even this is uncertain. Certainly the tide today is running against us as one statistic establishes. After the Second

World War in 1947, only 0.3 per cent of Australians declared themselves irreligious. Today, 22.3 per cent are without religion. The irreligiosity of most of Europe or the religious vitality of the United States, with some muted version of their culture wars, are our alternative Australian futures. Future generations will need much prayer, regular service, hard thinking and changes of attitude to build and maintain faith communities in the future.

My second preliminary point is to acknowledge that the Second Vatican Council is the twenty-first in Catholic history, in many ways completing the interrupted First Vatican Council (1869–70). As someone who stands with the recent popes in affirming a hermeneutic of continuity rather than seeing Vatican II as a doctrinal rupture or repudiation of earlier Councils, I do not go around proclaiming 'I am a Vatican Two priest' (although I am) because this is capable of misunderstanding, of fostering the illusion that the past is rejected. I am rather a priest of Jesus Christ, the head of the Church. I stand under the scriptures, under all the Councils and especially their creeds and am faithful to the Church's magisterial teaching.

I was a seminarian in Rome for the last three of the four conciliar sessions, arriving too late for the funeral of Pope John XXIII or the solemn inauguration of Pope Paul VI. It was 25 January 1959, when the much loved John XXIII announced, to general surprise and astonishment, that he would summon a new council to renew the religious life of the Church and bring her teachings, discipline and organization up to date. The unity of all Christians was its ultimate goal and the first session opened on 11 October 1962. Pope John died on 3 June 1963, and was succeeded by John Baptist Montini, then Archbishop of Milan, who took the name of Paul VI.

Pope John attributed the idea of convening the Council to a sudden inspiration of the Holy Spirit. As students, some of us surmised that the agent of the Holy Spirit's inspiration might have been the Jesuit priest and then Cardinal Agostino Bea, who was rector of the Pontifical Biblical Institute in Rome for nineteen years (1930–49). It therefore came as a surprise to me to read in Monsignor Georg Ratzinger's book on his brother the pope that Cardinal Joseph Frings, Archbishop of Cologne, had spoken openly about the possibility of a Council.[1] It was even more surprising to learn that on the eve of

---

[1]   Georg Ratzinger, *My Brother The Pope* (trans. Michael J. Miller; San Francisco: Ignatius Press, 2011), p. 189.

his election, Cardinal Roncalli was visited in his cell by Cardinals Ruffini and Ottaviani who suggested he convene a council; a suggestion he welcomed.[2] These two conservative cardinals had made a disastrous miscalculation that they would be able to control the assembled bishops in a brief council of a few months. Both Pius XI and Pius XII had examined the possibility of holding a council and decided not to do so.[3]

We have also learnt subsequently that soon after the convocation, Cardinal Montini of Milan, later to be the next pope, remarked in a telephone conversation that 'this holy old boy doesn't realize what a hornet's nest he's stirring up!'[4]

The surprise of many Church leaders shows that there was very little pressure for a Council even in Europe and almost none in Australia or indeed in the English-speaking world.

The devastation of the Second World War had wounded Europe terribly but churchgoing and missionary work overseas were high in countries like Holland, Ireland and Italy. However, in France, after more than 150 years of revolutions and wars, the exodus from the Church was under way and Roncalli had been nuncio there after the Second World War in a difficult period when de Gaulle felt the Church leadership had collaborated too much with the Pétainist regime under the Nazis.

The Council was saved by the accession of Pope Paul, who guided it through to a successful conclusion with the Council producing a number of truly excellent documents and realignments of Church life in conformity with the scriptures and the soundest tradition (more of that later).

Today, I would say that Pope John's intuition that the Church's old way of doing many things had developed from a vanished world and was no longer adequate was correct. I am not at all certain that the vital changes which the Council introduced, for example, the recognition of the role of the lay faithful, the collegiality of bishops, the importance of dialogue with the world rather than regular condemnation, the rejection of the state's power to coerce religious belief, ecumenism and celebrations of the liturgy in the vernacular (admittedly never proposed by the Council) – I am not sure these could have occurred without the Council.

---

2   Roberto de Mattei, *The Second Vatican Council (An Unwritten Story)* (trans. Patrick T. Brannan et al.; Fitzwilliam, NH: Loreto, English edition, 2012), pp. 96–97.
3   de Mattei, *The Second Vatican Council (An Unwritten Story)*, pp. 93–97.
4   Peter Hebblethwaite, *Paul VI: The First Modern Pope* (Mahweh, NJ: Paulist Press, 1993), p. 284.

Almost none of us can imagine returning to a world without ecumenism, because such Christian cooperation has transformed Australian public life and almost completely eliminated the ancient Catholic versus Protestant antagonisms. We cannot imagine celebrating all 'mixed marriages' (Catholic and non-Catholic) outside the Church in a sacristy, as was then required. Lay leadership is now exercised in all Catholic institutions except the parishes, which must be led by priests.

The parish priest is always the leader of the local community which he has to foster, developing truly Spirit-filled examples of 'communion' and where his celebration of the Eucharist is foundational together with his celebration of the other sacraments, especially the sacraments of reconciliation and baptism.

Sometimes a priest cannot reside in every local community, but since the priests share in the leadership roles of the bishops, they too are to be shepherds of their flock rather than being reduced to the role of sacramental providers or regarded as a school or hospital chaplain who is sometimes called on to contribute (and is sometimes not welcome).[5]

Christian participation in political life on both sides of the fence is more important than ever. The significant tension now is between a broad Jewish–Christian worldview and a pushy secularist minority who work to expand the possibilities of personal moral autonomy to the detriment of institutions such as marriage and the family (which provide the glue holding society together) and of values such as respect for the unborn and for the very old and sick.

Christians of the future will have a good number of children, which they will produce through personal acts of lovemaking (rather than breeding children as racehorses are bred today), and will refuse euthanasia. I expect also that in Australia a broadly based coalition, with many Gospel Christians from every denomination, will follow present patterns in the United States and reduce both the number of abortions and public approval for this awful practice.

One final point will complete this introductory section. During the Council and for some years afterwards I was confidently awaiting a new Pentecost. My first rebuff on that score came soon afterwards from a fellow post-graduate student in Oxford, an Anglican layman, older than myself and with a good deal of pastoral experience, who strongly pointed out how the tide was moving inexorably against us.

---

[5]   Paul VI, *Presbyterorum Ordinis* (7 December 1965), paras 2 and 6.

I was then reluctant to accept this point of view and in the light of subsequent events I now feel that my hopes were rather naïve. It was a small consolation to learn that the Council peritus of that time, Father Joseph Ratzinger, also believed there would be a new Pentecost, a new era in Church history.[6]

Whatever of that, it was a tonic as I prepared this paper to go over this old ground with a great deal of new information to relive the hopes and enthusiasms of those years. They were good times, even if they quickly turned sour and the revolutionary spirit of the sixties entered the Church. Some of my contemporaries consented to priestly ordination believing they would be allowed to marry later. More than 80 per cent of the Australian seminarians who studied in the years before and after my batch at Propaganda Fide College, Rome, either did not get ordained or left after ordination. They were the most talented group of Australian seminarians I had encountered (until recently). They worked productively in society, but were a big loss to the priesthood.

The Council itself

Pope Benedict has pointed out an important distinction that helps us understand what happened during the Council and especially after the Council. He distinguished between the 'true Council' and the 'Council of the media', between the real Council and what he called a virtual council. The true Council of the Fathers, as the bishop members of the Council were called, obviously moved within the faith tradition, but the Council of the journalists was seen through the categories of the secular media.

Benedict saw this as a political hermeneutic, or interpretation, where theological differences were reduced to power struggles and the press obviously sided with those who had more in common with their world. They worked for the decentralization of the Church, he said, where power was to be transferred from the pope to the bishops and then to popular sovereignty.[7]

With the invention of the pill, the sexual revolution and anti-children spirit which developed after this invention (values spread around the world by the music of groups such as the Beatles), the malaise from the Vietnam

---

[6] Benedict XVI, *Address to the clergy of Rome* (14 February 2013).
[7] Ibid.

War and the 1968 student uprisings in Europe, the virtual Council seemed more powerful than the real Council in much of the Western world for some decades until Pope John Paul II began his work. Pope Paul in 1972 spoke of 'the smoke of Satan entering the Church'.[8]

The atheist English writer Philip Larkin captures the spirit of those ingenuous times in his poem *Annus Mirabilis*. Two verses show this:

> Sexual intercourse began
> In nineteen sixty-three
> (which was rather late for me) -
> Between the end of the Chatterley ban
> And the Beatles first L.P.
> So life was never better than
> In nineteen sixty-three
> (Though just too late for me) -
> Between the end of the Chatterley ban
> And the Beatles first L.P.[9]

Lady Chatterley's Lover, a then notorious novel by the English writer D. H. Lawrence, had been banned from public sale for decades.

The progressive forces at the Council were much better at using the media and explaining and defending their point of view within the community of priests and seminarians. And the secular media was also adept at using these Church developments for their own purposes to undermine traditional authorities.

I still have in my files the documents which were regularly distributed to explain the different platforms of reform, which we accepted willingly as a basis for discussion and student argument.

Support for the programme of reform was almost unanimous among the huge seminarian population of Rome at the time. This enthusiasm was regularly undiscriminating, but soon after the Council's end, significant differences were emerging among even the students between those who followed the texts and those who used them as a springboard to appeal to the nebulous 'spirit of the Council'. We had thirty Australians at Propaganda Fide College when I arrived. This college on the Janiculum Hill had over

---

[8] Paul VI, Homily at the Mass in celebration of the IX anniversary of his papal coronation (29 June 1972).
[9] See Philip Larkin, 'Annus Mirabilis', in *High Windows* (London: Faber & Faber, 1974).

300 students from more than sixty nations and only 20 per cent of us were white or of European stock. I remain grateful for this marvellous experience. Australia was then still technically a mission country under the Congregation for the Propagation of the Faith and the bishops increased the number of Australians to sixty by around 1967 when I left Rome. As mentioned, the bishops 'lost' most of those men, some of whom were caught up in a rebellion at the College in 1968–69 and dispersed to the four winds around the globe. While a number of Australian priests continued to come to Rome after ordination for studies, it was about thirty years before Archbishop Hickey, Bishop Brennan and myself recommenced the tradition of sending some seminarians for study in Rome before ordination.

The currents of student opinion in Rome from the middle sixties through the seventies were almost exactly the opposite of what they are now, which today support doctrinal orthodoxy and liturgical orthopraxis.

Why was there such enthusiasm for change even among seminarians from countries where there had been little or no pressure for major reforms, where church practice was high and vocations plentiful? It is an interesting question especially when asked in the light of fifty years of experience since the Council started.

One factor was the immense popularity of Pope John XXIII who wanted a Council. Even more than today, Catholics then followed the Holy Father willingly. John generated huge enthusiasm outside as well as inside the Church, among churchgoers and fellow travellers. Our barber at my college (who came to us) was a plump and chatty Roman anti-clerical. He spoke fondly of the pope, calling him Papa Giovanni, while he always referred to Pope Pius XII as Papa Pacelli (his surname) and claimed the Holy Father had been more interested during the Second World War in preserving the Vatican Library than helping the Roman people. This was false and unjustified, but the man who made these false accusations liked Pope John.

Prosperity was returning to Europe, the opposing forces of the free world and communism had avoided world war over the 1963 Cuban crisis, and the presidency of J. F. Kennedy in the United States encouraged youthful self-confidence before his assassination. It was a time for optimism.

Another event took place in 1960, the Roman Synod, which Pope John convoked to examine the problems of the spiritual life of his own particular flock in the diocese of Rome. It seemed to escape completely from his control as it was stage-managed by the 'old guard'. It was a fiasco, as seminaries around the world were told that lectures should be delivered in Latin.

Already in Corpus Christi College (the Victorian seminary), and in most if not all other Australian seminaries, all the major text books in philosophy and theology were in Latin as were the oral exams. The first year in Rome when oral examinations could be taken in a language common to lecturer and student was 1967, two years after the close of the Council.

While it was one thing to have Latin texts, as well as the Latin Mass, lecturing in Latin was quite beyond the capacity of our lecturers in Werribee and certainly beyond the capacity of the unwilling listeners. A few lecturers attempted it and soon abandoned the project. Latin lectures, richly supplemented with Italian, continued during my years in Rome, but the attempt to universalize this custom was wildly unrealistic and a public relations disaster for the upcoming Council.

In fact it provided a salutary lesson, making the German and especially the French bishops determined that no such fate would befall the Council. Naturally enough, the English-speaking bishops, if for different reasons, strongly endorsed this stand.

The confrontation came early and was quickly resolved by majority vote. Pope John XXIII, like the Australian bishops, had hoped to conclude the Council by Christmas 1962.[10] They were to be disappointed. When Archbishop Achille Liénart of Lille, France, refused to be silenced by the president Cardinal Eugène Tisserant, and grabbed the microphone to announce that the proposed lists of consultors were unsatisfactory, he was backed by Cardinal Josef Frings who promised German support for his French colleague. In the face of increasing applause, Cardinal Tisserant closed the opening session.

It had lasted fifty minutes and was universally regarded as the crucial turning point. The bishops also went on to vote out the preliminary documents (schemata) and sent them back to be rewritten by new committees.

Lively dialogue continued, but the balance of power had changed as the bishops refused to be simply rubber stamps.

The most important document of the Council was the Dogmatic Constitution on the Church, *Lumen Gentium*, where a Copernican revolution

---

[10] de Mattei, *The Second Vatican Council (An Unwritten Story)*, p. 170.

saw the People of God (Chapter 2) treated before the hierarchy and episcopate (Chapter 3). The recognition of the baptismal dignity of the lay faithful was deeply in accord with the New Testament. It was also providential for the society that has emerged where hostile pressures have increased so much and effective resistance is quite beyond the capacity of the reduced number of clergy and religious. The Second Vatican Council recognized the proper dignity of the baptized.

Lumen Gentium also took up the interrupted work of the First Vatican Council and spelt out the role of all the bishops as successors of the Apostles, rather than delegates of the pope, in the doctrine of collegiality (the bishops ruling with and under Peter), which is classically exemplified in an Ecumenical Council and reflected in the regular Synods of Bishops. The creative tensions between the papacy and what Vatican II described as the College (not a biblical term) of Bishops, for example, the bishops with and under the pope and never without the pope, should be fruitful and interesting for Church life in this era of jet travel and instant communications.

The Pastoral Constitution on the Church in the World (*Gaudium et spes*) is one of the most controversial conciliar documents. Many, including Pope John Paul II, who helped prepare the document as a young bishop, felt it was too optimistic, taking insufficient account of original sin and the inevitable and constant battle between good and evil.

However, the basic doctrine that we engage with all those of good will, seek to cooperate rather than condemn, and participate regularly in the discussions of the Public Square are foundational attitudes for nearly every Catholic today. We were slow to acknowledge that we overestimated the Church's capacity for influence and underestimated the power of the different manifestations of the anti-Christ.

All in all, the Council produced sixteen documents, dogmatic constitutions, decrees and declarations on the major areas of church life. They vary in quality, so that the decrees on communications and the priesthood are not held in universally high regard, unlike the decree on the laity, probably influenced by input from Opus Dei, which followed on doctrinally from the constitution on the Church.

The Council set out to be pastoral rather than dogmatic, with the Council Fathers' opening address urging renewal, their ambition for the Church to be 'increasingly faithful to the gospel of Christ'. The two special issues they emphasized as important were peace, rather than war, and social justice, especially as it had been outlined in John XXIII's 1961 encyclical *Mater et Magistra*.[11]

At that stage, the Church was not confronted by any dramatic doctrinal challenges such as the nature of justification, or revelation, which were presented by the Protestant Reformation and dealt with at the Council of Trent.

Critics from both the left and the right reject a too literal following of the conciliar texts. Those of the left appealed to the 'spirit of the Council'. Those from the mainline right, like Father Divo Barsotti, an Italian mystic, insisted no Church renewal is possible without personal conversion. More particularly, the Italian traditionalist Professor Enrico Maria Radaelli lamented the pastoral language of the Council and the fact that the reverence due only to official dogmatic teaching is given to Vatican II's pastoral texts, so elevating them to unquestionable 'superdogmas'.[12] Both ends of the spectrum want some demythologizing.

There is something to be said for a few sharp anathemas, apart from the press coverage they would produce, because they strictly define and so limit the teachings to be rejected leaving the remainder of the field for productive theologizing. However, as Pope John Paul showed in his rejection of the ordination of women to the priesthood (1994) and his condemnation of abortion and euthanasia in Chapter 3 of *Evangelium Vitae* (1995), these teachings need to be simultaneously defended and explained.

The status of the particular teachings of Vatican II, as distinct from its major doctrines, will continue to produce discussion and differences within the Church.

Three other conciliar teachings deserve further attention because of their long term significance for Catholic life.

The least controversial of these is the Dogmatic Constitution on Revelation, *Dei Verbum*, which bypassed the explicit two-source theory of scripture and tradition. God is revealed through Jesus Christ, so that 'Sacred tradition

---

[11] John XXIII, Address on the occasion of the solemn opening of the most holy Council (11 October 1962), in *The Documents of Vatican II* (ed. W. M. Abbott S. J., 1966), pp. 3–7.

[12] Sandro Magister, 'The impossible "Road Map of Peace with the Lefebvrists"' (9 February 2013), *www.chiesa.espressonline.it.*

and sacred Scripture form one sacred deposit of the word of God, which is committed to the Church'. The teaching office is not above the Word of God. Tradition, scripture and the teaching authority of the Church are 'so linked and joined together that one cannot stand without the others' (*DV* 10).

This took a great deal of heat out of ecumenical discussion with Protestants and was the basis for the peaceful discussions and final document of the Synod on the Word of God (2008).

One could say that for the first time in English-speaking history, the Second Vatican Council encouraged Catholics to take the Bible to their heart. In some ways, the Old Testament was rediscovered, although the Bible stories of Adam and Eve, Abraham, Moses and the Exodus were well known.

Let me give three examples from this pre-conciliar and vanished world. Before the Second World War in the 1930s, in a small Irish-Australian parish near Ballarat where nearly everyone went to Sunday Mass, the paper boy would bring up the sporting newspaper for the weekend (called the *Sporting Globe*) to the Church for sale on Sunday morning. Many of the men left the Church during the sermon to go outside for a smoke and returned when the sermon was over.

The Bible belonged more to the Protestants with their strange notion of private judgement and we would refer to them, not always affectionately, as 'Bible Bashers'.

One nun with whom I worked closely in Catholic teacher education, only about fifteen years older than myself, told me that when she was in training as a nun they were not allowed to have a New Testament, let alone a whole Bible.

We did study the Gospel in my senior secondary school years in the late 1950s.

In a different way, the Declaration on Religious Freedom *Dignitatis Humanae* (1965) was the catalyst for the schism of the Lefebvrists (but not their only point of difficulty) with its teaching that religious people have 'immunity from coercion in civil society' (*DH* 1). This doctrine, that the state cannot compel religious belief ties in well with our English-speaking concept of religious freedom, and will be even more important in the future if governments follow the Obama line and try to reduce freedom of religion to a freedom to worship privately and remove religious considerations from public discussion and public life.

The distinguished American theologian, Father John Courtney Murray S. J., who made a major contribution to the development of this declaration, acknowledged it as 'the most controversial document of the whole Council'. He also wrote that 'the conciliar affirmation of the principle of freedom was narrowly limited in the text. But the text itself was flung into a pool whose shores are as wide as the universal Church. The ripples will run far.'[13]

He was right, because some have jumped from this proper recognition of the limited power of the state in terms of religious coercion (compelling belief or practice) to a damaging affirmation of the primacy of conscience, which at its worst enables Christians to select from official Christian teaching on faith and morals only those doctrines they find congenial. The more cautious speak of the priority of the informed conscience, but conscience stands under truth and the Word of God, not above it. As Cardinal Newman wrote, conscience is 'the aboriginal vicar of Christ' and 'a messenger from him, who …, speaks to us behind a veil, and teaches and rules us by his representatives.'[14]

He also explained with complete accuracy that 'conscience is the highest of teachers, yet the least luminous ... so easily puzzled, obscured, perverted ... so biased by pride and passion'.[15]

My third point touches on the Constitution on the Sacred Liturgy which was, with the decree on social communications, the first document promulgated by the Council on 4 December 1963.

In many ways, it is a beautiful piece of work where the Paschal Mystery, the suffering, death and resurrection of the Lord, is placed at the heart of the Eucharist. The liturgy is the fountain of the Church's power and the summit of her activity.[16] It encouraged the *participatio actuosa* of all the people in the liturgy which some saw as an alternative to prayer and especially silent prayer.[17] It endorsed 'noble simplicity' and a 'general restoration of the liturgy itself', authorizing changes to both 'texts and rites'.[18]

The document is modest enough and it has been claimed that Pope John only envisaged some parts of the Mass in the vernacular. But the Council's

---

[13] John Courtney Murray, S. J., in W. M. Abbott, S. J., *Documents of Vatican II* (1966), pp. 672–764.
[14] John Henry Newman, 'Letter to the Duke of Norfolk', in *The Genius of John Henry Newman: Selections from his Writings* (Oxford: Clarendon Press, 1989), pp. 263–64. Cf. *Catechism of the Catholic Church* (London: Burns & Oates, 1994), par. 1778.
[15] Newman, 'Letter to the Duke of Norfolk', pp. 253–54.
[16] Paul VI, *Sacrosanctum Concilium* (4 December 1963), par. 10.
[17] Ibid., par. 15.
[18] Ibid., paras 34, 21.

Commission on the Liturgy, under Cardinal Giacomo Lercaro of Bologna, pushed forward energetically. If I could lapse into an Australian metaphor, the liturgical horse bolted as the spirit of the world penetrated deeply.

We escaped the worst of it here in Australia. There are still geographical pockets in Europe where the official Eucharistic prayers are used only rarely.

Under Pope Benedict, considerable progress was made in strengthening the transcendental dimension of worship. He has been very explicit about the damage done, saying that 'these translations, trivializations of the idea of the Council were virulent in the praxis of the application of liturgical reform'.[19]

Liturgy, in Benedict's words, came to be seen by some as a 'community activity, a profane matter' and not an act of faith. Sacrality was seen as pagan. Christ died outside the gates, in the profane world, and therefore liturgy is not seen as an act of worship, but of profane participation, where participation was reduced to activity.

For a long time, I did not understand deeply enough the damaging consequences in Catholic life of bad liturgy. Sloppy, irreverent horizontalism, the downgrading of the vertical dimension, and no longer striving towards the Transcendent are all an unfailing expression of spiritual malaise. 'Shonky' liturgy facilitated the introduction and acceptance of defective religious education texts (and vice versa).

If the fruits of the conciliar reforms are to be realized and if the work of the Spirit is to produce more and better fruit, we must continue to see the sacraments and especially the Mass as expressions of faithful and reverent worship.

Unfortunately for many in Australia, Sunday is no longer a day of rest and sport on Sunday morning is a regular deterrent to worship for children. None of this helps.

After the Council

None of us would be at ease if we tried to return to a time before Vatican II. We are all happy with lay leadership in most areas of church service, for example,

---

[19] Benedict XVI, *Address to the clergy of Rome* (14 February 2013).

health, education, welfare, aged care. Ecumenical cooperation is a theological imperative and a strategic necessity to resist hostile secularism. Despite the proper enthusiasm of a number of faithful for the Tridentine Mass, celebrated in Latin of course, the overwhelming majority prefer the liturgy in the vernacular, the language they understand. The separation of Church and state, implicit in the rejection of the state's power to coerce religious belief and practice, not only respects personal freedom, but will be a useful defence if pressures against religious liberty continue and increase. It is now accepted that we have parish finance councils and that bishops from around the world participate on the councils of the curial departments and that the curia should have priests and religious from around the world in their ranks.

The Council brought and brings us many blessings and changes which benefit Church communities, but many unexpected developments also occurred. There were plenty of surprises.

No one expected the phenomenal growth of the Pentecostal communities (or sects), which are now the fourth largest religious grouping in the world. They are particularly strong in South and Central America among Protestants, while the Catholic Church in Brazil has a vibrant Catholic charismatic constituency.

No one predicted the growth of a community such as the Neo-Catechumenal Way, which in just over forty years has grown to 1,400,000 members and runs more than seventy seminaries throughout the world, including one in the Sydney archdiocese.

I did not predict the doctrinal and moral confusion that developed, as largely secular majority views in Australian society penetrated into Catholic hearts and minds. I remember an older lady whose son was proposing to marry a woman who was leaving her husband, telling me that the Church was likely to approve such adultery in the future as so many things had already changed, such as the language of the Mass.

This confusion was particularly marked in the understanding of sexual morality, marriage and family, where the 1968 teaching of Pope Paul VI in *Humanae Vitae* against artificial contraception was rejected and continues to be widely rejected. In 1994, Pope John Paul II spoke of a true crisis in moral understanding (*Veritatis Splendor* 93) with confusion spreading from contraception to abortion, euthanasia and same-sex marriages.

In a similar way, no one I knew anticipated the scourge of juvenile sexual abuse which would be uncovered and seems to have peaked in the 1970s–80s when, incidentally, moral confusion was at its height.

I never encountered anyone during or soon after the Council who predicted the waves of departures from the priesthood and religious life, the eventual extinction of many religious orders and the drying up of vocations.

My figures are not comprehensive, but I believe they are not unrepresentative. One estimate has it that 10,000 priests from around the world left during the pontificate of Pope Paul VI (1963–78). In Australia, there were 14,662 nuns in 1966, but only 4,765 last year with a median age of seventy-four. During the years of the Council, 1962–65, approximately sixty seminarians entered each year at Springwood for New South Wales and ACT. Last year, we had eighty-three seminarians altogether for NSW and ACT, which represents a substantial increase on the numbers in the early 1990s. While the Nashville Dominican Sisters who came to Sydney before WYD in 2007 have accepted nine Australian young women with two more coming in August since then, most orders of nuns have only a few vocations. Between 1997 and 2008, 268 women became nuns and about forty have since resigned.

The piety in the Sydney archdiocese remains somewhat more traditional than in Melbourne. One only has to examine the interiors of their two beautiful cathedrals to identify a difference of tone.

However, to varying degrees right across Australia, parishes saw a Protestant-type removal of many statues, monstrances and candlesticks. Simplicity was the aim, even when noble simplicity was elusive.

One apocryphal story from country Victoria tells of a country priest who decided to dump his church statues in a neighbouring lake. To his consternation, he discovered that they refused to sink, remaining obdurately on the surface. He had to return to his presbytery for his rifle and put a few bullets into them to obtain his desired effect!

Those days are now gone – largely if not completely, due principally to the leadership of Pope John Paul II and Pope Benedict. I never anticipated that fifty years after the beginning of the Council that my strongly liberal and theologically radical seminarian friends would have almost no successors among the seminarians of today in the English-speaking world.

Immediately after the Council, when medieval devotions were fiercely resisted and largely uncelebrated, it would have been impossible for me or any of my fellow Roman seminarians to have imagined the popularity of silent prayer before the Blessed Sacrament among many young adults, their fondness for Benediction, or that we would have at least 5,000 people each year at our Corpus Christi procession. Neither would we have imagined that a Synod on the Eucharist in 2010 would conclude with a Holy Hour and Benediction with the Holy Father and all the Synod members. Pope John Paul had to overcome strong opposition to start the World Youth Days. No one then dreamt of 400,000 at a Youth Mass in Sydney, 2,000,000 in Rome in 2000 and similar numbers at Rio de Janeiro led by a charismatic Jesuit pope from Argentina in 2013, who had been a determined opponent of liberation theology and a champion of the poor and marginalized. God writes straight in crooked lines, but God is always with us.

All priests and religious love the Church, as they love Christ, even (or perhaps especially) when they differ about what the Church needs.

Some still cling to the belief that if we just make ourselves a bit more reasonable, a bit less demanding and a bit more up to date, then big numbers will come into the Church. However, statistics show that the more liberal the Church community, the faster the exodus.

Unfortunately, too many lapsed into a contraceptive Christianity, where nearly everything appears normal on the surface, but is unable to produce new life.

In contraceptive Christianity, God is underplayed, sacrifice is not mentioned, repentance and forgiveness are not required and everyone has the right to happiness in heaven or perhaps to a convenient annihilation. Even Jesus can become like Harry Potter's foe Voldemort: 'He who must not be named.' This is nowhere good enough. The one true God and his Son deserve much better. Certainly the Second Vatican Council neither recommended nor silently condoned such a write-down, such a retreat from the call to repent and believe.

These few words on Vatican II for the world of today and tomorrow might not be sufficiently optimistic for some, perhaps too pessimistic. We are called to neither of these alternatives, but to realism and the Christian virtue of hope, which is quite different from a facile optimism. There are many signs of hope.

Let me conclude with a quotation I have used on a number of occasions from G. K. Chesterton's small masterpiece, *Orthodoxy: The Romance of Faith*.

Chesterton wrote that the Catholic Church is a lion tamer, which goes in for dangerous ideas. Christians are not a flock of sheep 'but a herd of bulls and tigers, of terrible ideals and devouring doctrines, which can degenerate into a false religion and lay waste the world'.[20]

The Church has to go on her way very carefully because 'she is a great and daring experiment of irregular equilibrium'.

Following Christ in the Catholic tradition is thrilling and exciting, but perilous when we get things wrong. In every age there are obstacles and traps, Chesterton wrote. And as he puts it:

> To have fallen into any of those open traps of error and exaggeration ... – that would indeed have been simple. It is always simple to fall; there are an infinity of angles at which one falls, only one at which one stands. To have fallen into any one of the fads ... would indeed have been obvious and tame. But to have avoided them all has been one whirling adventure; and in my vision the heavenly chariot flies thundering through the ages, the dull heresies sprawling and prostrate, the wild truth reeling but erect.

So be it.

---

[20] G. K. Chesterton, *Orthodoxy: The Romance of Faith* (Doubleday Books, 1959), pp. 100–01.

2

Communio: The Key to Vatican II's Ecclesiology

Marc Cardinal Ouellet PSS

Fifty years after the opening of the Second Vatican Council, the Church can better gauge the scope of this event and the import of its texts, which profoundly marked her life and her relation to the world at the turn of the third millennium.

St John XXIII set two main goals for the Council: to bring the presentation of the Church's doctrine up to date and to promote the unity of Christians.[1] These two objectives were intended to renew the Church's relation with the modern world and thus to give a new impetus to her universal mission.

In order to attain these objectives, the Council Fathers undertook a fundamental reflection on ecclesiology, in the hopes of better defining the Church's profound nature, her essential structure and the meaning of her mission in a world increasingly emancipated from her influence and tradition. The rise of liberalism and various forms of nationalism in nineteenth-century Europe created a climate of confrontation between the Church and the modern world. In this context, Vatican Council I defined the dogma of papal infallibility. The complementary theme of episcopal collegiality remained undeveloped because of the Franco-Prussian War, which caused the suspension of the Council.

After the tragedies of the twentieth century, the Church had to take up the elaboration of this doctrine once more. Above all, she had to reconstruct the bridges connecting her to the modern world. Vatican Council II responded to these needs by renewing ecclesiology as a whole, and by laying the foundations for the evangelization of the third millennium.

---

[1] John XXIII, Address on the occasion of the solemn opening of the most holy Council (11 October 1962).

Since the Extraordinary Synod of 1985, celebrating the twentieth anniversary of the closing of the Council, the idea of communion has become the dominant interpretation of the Council's ecclesiology.[2] This positive orientation, very promising from an ecumenical and pastoral perspective, has had a great deal of success. However, it has also given rise to superficial and ideological interpretations. At a conference in November 2000, Cardinal Joseph Ratzinger made this incisive judgement:

> The Second Vatican Council clearly wanted to speak of the Church within the discourse on God, to subordinate the discourse on the Church to the discourse on God and to offer an ecclesiology that would be theo-logical in a true sense. Until now, however, the way the Council was received has ignored this qualifying characteristic in favor of individual ecclesiological affirmations; it has highlighted single phrases that are easy to repeat, and has thus fallen away from the broad horizons of the Council Fathers.[3]

He confirmed this criticism by observing that the first document promulgated by the Council was the Constitution on the Sacred Liturgy. In the architecture of the Council, this order had a precise sense: 'Adoration comes first. Therefore God comes first. … In the history of the post-Conciliar period, the Constitution on the Liturgy was certainly no longer understood from the viewpoint of the basic primacy of adoration, but rather as a recipe book of what we can do with the Liturgy.'[4]

We have to recognize the truth of this criticism, at least in certain milieus in which forgetfulness of God encouraged a tendency to change everything that could be changed in the liturgy, without much concern for pedagogy. Consequently, the sacred meaning of the liturgy and its theandric character were more or less lost, replaced by the activity of the community and its ministers. The particular ecclesiological issues we mentioned earlier, for example, the relation between the universal Church and the particular

---

[2]   'The ecclesiology of communion is the central and fundamental idea of the documents of the Council' (Second General Assembly, Extraordinary Synod of Bishops, *Ecclesia sub Verbo Dei Mysteria Christi Celebrans pro Salute Mundi. Relatio Finalis*, 1985, II.C.1). Cf. also: Manuel Sánchez Monge, *Eclesiología. La iglesia, misterio de comunión y misión* (Madrid: Sociedad de educación Atenas, 1994); Dennis M. Doyle, *Communion Ecclesiology: Vision and Versions* (Maryknoll, NY: Orbis Books, 2000); Jean-Marie Roger Tillard, *Église d'Églises: L'ecclésiologie de communion* (Paris: Cerf, 1987).

[3]   Joseph Ratzinger, 'The Ecclesiology of the Constitution of the Church, Vatican II, *Lumen Gentium*' (November 2000), http://www.ewtn.com/library/CURIA/CDFECCL.HTM. English translation from *L'Osservatore Romano*, Weekly Edition in English (19 September 2001), p. 5.

[4]   Ratzinger, 'The Ecclesiology of the Constitution of the Church, Vatican II, *Lumen Gentium*', p. 5.

churches, the primacy of the pope and episcopal collegiality, the relation between institution and charisms, and democratic models of communion took centre stage, but they were not treated with the requisite theological depth. Hence Cardinal Ratzinger's – Pope Benedict XVI's – powerful call to deepen our understanding of the Council's ecclesiology in the light of what the same Council says about God.

The time has thus come to reread the Second Vatican Council without ideological prejudice, with the intention of further developing its ecclesiology of communion. This ecclesiology is not, after all, a completed endeavour in the Council's texts.[5] Thus, I propose first to point out the steps that led to the ecclesiology of communion; second, to clarify its theological foundation; and finally, to suggest a few concluding perspectives for the further development of particular questions.

Conciliar milestones: Towards an ecclesiology of communion

When we look back at the event of the Council and everything that followed it, we are still struck by its newness, as well as its effects in the Church's life and mission. Though we cannot ignore the problems in interpretation or the phenomena of regression, we must greet the Council as a new Pentecost that reawakened the Church's missionary consciousness. It granted her a vision and doctrinal orientation that allowed for a renewal of her structures and pastoral activity.

To my mind, the Council's most obvious novelties were its reform of the liturgy, the development of an understanding of episcopal collegiality, the universal call to holiness, ecumenical commitment, a strong promotion of the apostolate of the laity, and an opening to religious freedom and to inter-religious dialogue. All of these reveal a new spirit and new attitudes, rooted in a more lively awareness of the Church's nature and mission. I mention here a few milestones in this new awareness.

---

[5] Ibid. 'It should be recognized first of all that the word *communio* does not have a central position in the Council. But if it is properly understood it can serve as a synthesis for the essential elements of conciliar ecclesiology.'

Liturgical reform

As we noted the first document promulgated by the Council Fathers promoted a reform of the liturgy. We can assess the application of this reform differently in different milieus, but its central objective was entirely legitimate and necessary: the 'conscious and active participation of the faithful' in the Holy Eucharist. The Constitution *Sacrosanctum Concilium* defines the holy liturgy as 'an exercise of the priestly office of Jesus Christ', to which the Church is associated as his body and beloved bride. This action, the Council Fathers recognized, is 'the source and summit' of the Church's life: 'Every liturgical celebration … is a sacred action surpassing all others; no other action of the Church can equal its efficacy by the same title and to the same degree' (*SC* 7). The life of the Church was profoundly transformed by this active and conscious participation of the faithful, which nourished their spiritual life and prompted their apostolic and social commitment. This is why we must consider the liturgical reform, its limits notwithstanding, as a first great milestone in the journey towards an ecclesiology of communion.

Episcopal collegiality

A second great milestone in this journey was the doctrinal development of 'the hierarchical structure of the Church and in particular … the episcopate' (*LG*, ch. 3). The relations between the primacy of the successor of Peter and the collegiality of bishops, the successors of the Apostles, had to be balanced and harmonized in order to correspond to the true nature of the Church as willed by Christ.

From the Church's beginning, the institution of the Twelve and its continuation in the apostolic succession assures the sacramental permanence of Christ as the supreme pontiff in the midst of his people. Through the mediation of the Apostles and their successors, Christ continues to exercise his threefold function of teaching, sanctifying and governing his people. Bishops exercise their pastoral ministry in the particular Church assigned to them, while sharing in responsibility for the universal Church because they belong to the College of Bishops. The exercise of this universal responsibility, in strict episcopal collegiality, above all regards participation in Councils or Synods. But in the less juridical form of the *affectus collegialis*, it also regards Bishops' Conferences and all the various forms of pastoral collaboration between the bishops of a region, country or continent.

This spirit of communion promoted by the Council gave rise to other structures of participation on a local level, such as presbyteral councils, diocesan or parish pastoral councils, and public or private associations of the faithful, which encourage various forms of apostolate and fraternal relations between the members of an ecclesial family.

The unity of Christians

We recall that one of the Council's original goals was the restoration of unity between divided Christians. Ecumenical encounters and dialogue, cultivated during and after the Council, significantly contributed to the emergence of the ecclesiology of communion. On a theological level, we must highlight the fact that the Eucharistic ecclesiology of certain Orthodox authors in fact introduced the idea of *koinonia-communio* into conciliar ecclesiology.[6] This idea subsequently became the central theme of the ecclesiology of communion, thanks to the dialogue between Catholic and Orthodox theologians.[7]

But beyond the particular discussions, ecumenism brought the Trinitarian foundation of unity back to the fore. The Decree on Ecumenism summarizes from a Catholic viewpoint the perspective of unity that results from this foundation:

> It is the Holy Spirit, dwelling in those who believe and pervading and ruling over the Church as a whole, who brings about that wonderful communion of the faithful. He brings them into intimate union with Christ, so that He is the principle of the Church's unity. … This is the sacred mystery of the unity of the Church, in Christ and through Christ, the Holy Spirit energizing its

---

6   Cf. Nicolas Afanassieff, *L'Église du Saint-Esprit* (Paris: Cerf, 1975); Jean Zizioulas, *L'être ecclésial* (Geneva: Labor et Fides, 1981).

7   Walter Kasper, 'Ecclésiologie eucharistique: de Vatican II à l'exhortation Sacramentum Caritatis', in *L'Eucharistie, don de Dieu pour la vie du monde. Actes du Symposium international de théologie* (Ottawa: CECC, 2009), pp. 194–95.

various functions. It is a mystery that finds its highest exemplar and source in the unity of the Persons of the Trinity: the Father and the Son in the Holy Spirit, one God. (*UR* 2)

The anthropology of the *imago Dei*

A fourth important milestone on the path towards an ecclesiology of communion seems to me to be the anthropology of the *imago Dei*, the image of God, which forms the basic framework of the Pastoral Constitution *Gaudium et spes*. This document is based on a renewed vision of human dignity in Christ (*GS* 22). It highlights the divine vocation of the human person, which is expressed in terms of the gift of self in the image of God: 'The Lord Jesus, when he prayed to the Father … implied a certain likeness between the union of the divine Persons, and the unity of God's sons in truth and charity. This likeness reveals that man, who is the only creature on earth which God willed for itself, cannot fully find himself except through a sincere gift of himself' (*GS* 24).

This anthropology includes a renewed vision of marriage and the family. This 'intimate partnership of … life and love' (*GS* 48) is blessed and as it were consecrated by the Holy Spirit, thus attaining to the dignity of the 'domestic church' (*LG* 11). Pope John Paul II amply developed this conciliar intuition regarding the domestic Church, which extends *koinonia-communio* into the first cell of ecclesial and social life.

Alongside these milestones, which are points of light, we cannot ignore certain shadows, which have made the implementation of the Council's orientations in the direction of *communio* more difficult. Along with the liturgical abuses and purely horizontal interpretations of the ecclesiology of communion we mentioned at the outset, there was the debate regarding the encyclical *Humanae Vitae*. Such dissension was not conducive to the serene reception of the Council's anthropology and its ethical consequences.

These shadows reveal a crisis of faith that hindered the right reception and interpretation of the Council. Both traditionalists and progressives spoke of a rupture with the tradition, whether their intent was to reject the Council wholesale and retreat into schism or to give it a 'liberal' sense that would allow the cultural currents of the age to drag the Church along in their wake.

Although these false interpretations are limited, they have had a real influence for decades – so much so that Pope Benedict XVI thought it necessary to clarify the hermeneutic of the Council at the beginning of his pontificate.[8] His important address to the Roman Curia in December 2005 took up with greater authority Cardinal Ratzinger's Jubilee Year observations on the ecclesiology of communion. As we have seen, in that earlier text, he had stressed the divine and universal dimension of the Church in order to correct superficial interpretations of ecclesial communion.[9]

Now that we have considered these conciliar milestones, we must root the ecclesiology of communion in the Council's most fundamental texts.

The conciliar foundations for an ecclesiology of communion

1 The Christological foundation

The emergence of an ecclesiology of communion is tied to the Council's reflection on the liturgy, ecumenism and anthropology. But the foundation of this ecclesiology depends above all on the Council's Christocentric orientation, which we will evoke, taking the great conciliar Constitutions as our starting point. We will begin by looking at the way the Council treated divine revelation:

> Hearing the word of God with reverence and proclaiming it with faith, the sacred synod takes its direction from these words of St. John: 'We announce to you the eternal life which dwelt with the Father and was made visible to us. What we have seen and heard we announce to you, so that you may have fellowship with us and our common fellowship be with the Father and His Son Jesus Christ.' (1 Jn 1.2-3). (*DV* 2)

Without a doubt, this passage from the first letter of John cited in the preface of the Constitution *Dei Verbum* expresses the Council's dominant inspiration, the biblical source that gives the tone and the method for a deeper doctrinal

---

[8] Benedict XVI, *Address to the Roman Curia on the occasion of the traditional exchange of Christmas greetings* (22 December 2005).

[9] Ratzinger, 'The Ecclesiology of the Constitution of the Church, Vatican II, *Lumen Gentium*'. Cf. also Congregation for the Doctrine of the Faith, *Communionis Notio* [Letter to the Bishops of the Catholic Church on Some Aspects of the Church Understood as Communion], 28 May 1992.

understanding of revelation and the Church. In a way, this Johannine text dictates the method of divine revelation from its content. What is John saying to us? He speaks of eternal life, which must be announced from the experience of an authentic participation in the Trinitarian communion. Taking its inspiration from this passage, and without ignoring the noetic dimension of the 'truths of revelation', *Dei Verbum* stresses the personal and dynamic dimension of this revelation: 'In His goodness and wisdom God chose to reveal Himself and to make known to us the hidden purpose of His will (see Eph. 1.9) by which through Christ, the Word made flesh, man might in the Holy Spirit have access to the Father and come to share in the divine nature' (see Eph. 2.18; 2 Pet. 1.4). This personal dimension is explained through its modalities of communication: familiar conversation and welcome. 'Through this revelation, therefore, the invisible God (see Col. 1.15, 1 Tim. 1.17) out of the abundance of His love speaks to men as friends (see Ex. 33.11; Jn 15.14-15) and lives among them (see Bar. 3.38), so that He may invite and take them into fellowship with Himself' (*DV* 2).

In fact, the Council not only renews the theology of revelation in the light of Christ, 'who is both the mediator and the fullness of all revelation' (*DV* 2); it also renews our manner of presenting the faith. Faith means adhering personally to someone who invites us to enter into His communion. This is significant progress with respect to the preceding scholastic approach, which expressed itself in terms of intellectual assent to abstract truths. The Council's Christocentric and Trinitarian perspective on revelation, enriched by a more personalist language, represents a turning point that confers on the Dogmatic Constitution *Dei Verbum* pride of place as the foundation of conciliar ecclesiology.

This same Christological foundation appears in the first sentence of the Constitution on the Church, *Lumen Gentium*: 'Christ is the Light of nations. Because this is so, this Sacred Synod gathered together in the Holy Spirit eagerly desires, by proclaiming the Gospel to every creature (cf. Mk 16.15), to bring the light of Christ to all men, a light brightly visible on the countenance of the Church' (*LG* 1). We note that from the beginning, the document speaks of the Church as a person, whose 'countenance' reflects Christ's light.

This opening sentence is followed by the guiding idea, which seeks to define the profound nature of the Church as well as her relationship to the world:

'The Church is in Christ like a sacrament or as a sign and instrument both of a very closely knit union with God and of the unity of the whole human race' (*LG* 1). We are familiar with the idea of sacrament when it refers to the seven sacraments, but it is a great novelty to apply this term, even analogically, to the Church as such. A certain theological reflection of biblical and liturgical inspiration prepared the ground for this broadening of the notion of sacrament, but it was the Council that introduced this new perspective, which profoundly changes our understanding of the Church and her mission.[10] We must take stock of this novelty, which is at the basis of the ecclesiology of communion.

2 The sacramental nature of the Church

The first chapter of *Lumen Gentium* presents the mystery of the Church, the universal sacrament of salvation, beginning from the role proper to each of the three divine persons in the plan of salvation. This Trinitarian perspective allows us to broaden the notion of sacrament to include the Church, understood in continuity with the Incarnation of the Word and in profound synergy with the mission of the Holy Spirit. In paragraphs inspired by the Holy Spirit, the Council then highlights the sacramental foundation of the ecclesiology of communion. Baptism and the Eucharist together incorporate us into Christ:

> Through Baptism we are formed in the likeness of Christ: 'For in one Spirit we were all baptized into one body.' ... Really partaking of the body of the Lord in the breaking of the Eucharistic bread, we are taken up into communion with Him and with one another. 'Because the bread is one, we though many, are one body, all of us who partake of the one bread.' In this way all of us are made members of His Body, 'but individually members one of another'. (*LG* 7)

Contemporary exegesis of 1 Corinthians 10.16-17 made a substantial contribution to the ecclesiology of communion by stressing once again the ecclesial meaning of Eucharistic communion.[11] According to St Paul, communion in

---

[10] Cf. Edward Schillebeeckx, *Christ the Sacrament of the Encounter with God* (Sheed & Ward, 1987); Otto Semmelroth, *Die Kirche als Ursakrament* (Frankfurt a.M.: Knecht, 1955).

[11] Cf. Xavier Léon-Dufour, 'Corps du Christ et Eucharistie selon saint Paul', in *Le corps et le corps du Christ dans la première Épître aux Corinthiens* (*Congrès de l'ACFEB, Tarbes, 1981*) (Paris: Cerf, 1983), pp. 225–55; Hervé Legrand, 'Communion eucharistique et communion ecclésiale. Une relecture de la première lettre aux Corinthiens', *Centro Pro Unione Bulletin* 67 (Spring 2005), pp. 21–32.

Christ's Eucharistic body builds up the Church as the Body of Christ. For the celebration of the Eucharist actualizes the mystery of the Covenant, that is, the total gift that Christ made of his body to his bride, the Church. He did this to sanctify and nourish her (cf. Eph. 5.27ff.) and to associate her to his own fruitfulness, for the world's salvation (cf. *LG* 7). From this baptismal and Eucharistic foundation, the Council deepens our understanding of the Church's sacramental nature in the light of the incarnate Word:

> By no weak analogy, [the Church] is compared to the mystery of the incarnate Word. As the assumed nature inseparably united to Him, serves the divine Word as a living organ of salvation, so, in a similar way, does the visible social structure of the Church serve the Spirit of Christ, who vivifies it, in the building up of the body. This is the one Church of Christ which in the Creed is professed as one, holy, catholic and apostolic, which our Savior, after His Resurrection, commissioned Peter to shepherd. (*LG* 8)

We are here in the presence of a fundamental text for the ecclesiology of communion. *Lumen Gentium* 8 presents us with an analogy, of course, but one that profoundly grasps the sacramental nature of the Church and her mission. A sacrament is defined as a visible sign of an invisible grace; it consists of a human and a divine element, as inseparable as the two natures of the incarnate Word. The Church is constituted as a sacrament by a visible body and an invisible Spirit, who animates it. This Spirit acts and expresses himself through the community of his members. The ensuing spiritual community is hierarchically ordered and placed under the authority of Peter and the other Apostles. The Church is thus a mysterious subject who is at once divine and human; as Thomas Aquinas says, she is a mystical person.[12] She is certainly a community, but this community is unified and personalized by the Spirit of Christ, who animates it.

On the basis of the Church's sacramental nature, the ecclesiology of communion can thus ask not only, '*What* is the Church?', but '*Who* is the Church?' For the sacramental nature we just described points first to the Holy Spirit, who animates and constitutes the Church as the Body of Christ. Suddenly, the Church in her mystery appears above all as a person, a Trinitarian

---

[12] '... caput et membra sunt quasi una persona mystica': *Summa theologiae*, IIIª pars, q. 48, a. 2, ad 1; Cf. Heribert Mühlen, *L'Esprit dans l'Église: Una Mystica persona* (Paris: Cerf, 1969).

presence who lives and acts in a human institution. This community, humanly 'personalized' in Mary, is unified through the communion of the divine persons. This divine communion dwells in the Church and confers on her a sacramental dignity – that is to say, her worth as 'a sign and instrument both of a very closely knit union with God and of the unity of the whole human race' (*LG* 1).

The People of God

In Chapter 2 of the Constitution *Lumen Gentium*, the notion of the Church-sacrament is completed by that of the People of God. For 'God … does not make men holy and save them merely as individuals, without bond or link between one another. Rather has it pleased Him to bring men together as one people, a people which acknowledges Him in truth and serves Him in holiness' (*LG* 9). This is a 'messianic people … established by Christ as a communion of life, charity and truth, it is also used by Him as an instrument for the redemption of all' (*LG* 9).

Such a communitarian perspective develops the notion of the Church-sacrament in the direction of communion, understood in its Trinitarian depth and its universal extension. The term 'People of God' in fact implies a horizontal component of social organization and a vertical component of the community's participation in Christ's priesthood. Both components are to be understood in the light of the sacramental realism of the Eucharist, which falls on the relation between the members of Christ's Body and on the apostolic and missionary activities of the Church.

We note how *Lumen Gentium* introduces the notion of the priesthood in this context: 'Christ the Lord, High Priest taken from among men, made the new people "a kingdom of priests to God, his Father."' The Council speaks first of a common priesthood of the baptized, who 'are consecrated as a spiritual house and a holy priesthood, in order that … they may offer spiritual sacrifices'. This priesthood is exercised 'through all those works which are those of the Christian' (*LG* 10): prayer of praise and thanksgiving, sacrifices, the witness of a holy life, self-abnegation and active charity.

The basic structure of the new People of God willed by Christ the Lord is thus the community of the baptized, who form a 'kingdom of priests to

God, his Father.' The ministerial or hierarchical priesthood comes in second place, as a service to this priestly community. *Lumen Gentium* takes care to clarify, however, that 'though they differ from one another in essence and not only in degree, the common priesthood of the faithful and the ministerial or hierarchical priesthood are nonetheless interrelated: each of them in its own special way is a participation in the one priesthood of Christ' (*LG* 10).

It is thus through the joint exercise of these two modes of participation in the one priesthood of Christ that the Church accomplishes her sacramental mediation vis-à-vis the world. This sacramental mediation rests as a whole upon the spiritual maternity of Mary, who, through her most intimate union with Christ the Redeemer, gives birth to and accompanies the two forms of participation in her Son's one priesthood. The Virgin, model par excellence of faith and fidelity to the Holy Spirit, intercedes for us so that the fruitful union of all the members of Christ's Body and the universal missionary dynamism of the Church gradually lead human history to its eschatological fulfilment. This is the global perspective of the Church's sacramentality, which forms the basis of the ecclesiology of communion.

The fundamental texts we have evoked allow us to perceive the 'theological' nature of the Council's ecclesiology, as well as the pertinence of Cardinal Ratzinger's Jubilee Year appeal:

> The first sentence of the Constitution on the Church immediately explains that the Council does not consider the Church as a reality closed in on herself, but sees her in a Christological perspective: 'Christ is the light of the nations; and it is, accordingly, the heartfelt desire of this sacred Council … that … the light of Christ, reflected on the face of the Church, may enlighten all men.' With this background we can understand the image used in the theology of the Fathers, who see the Church as the moon that does not shine with its own light, but reflects the light of Christ the sun. Ecclesiology is shown to be dependent upon Christology and connected with it. But since no one can speak correctly of Christ, of the Son, without at the same time speaking of the Father, and, since it is impossible to speak correctly of the Father and the Son without listening to the Holy Spirit, the Christological vision of the Church necessarily expands to become a Trinitarian ecclesiology (*LG* 2–4). The discourse on the Church is a discourse on God, and only in this way is it correct.[13]

---

[13] Ratzinger, 'The Ecclesiology of the Constitution of the Church, Vatican II, *Lumen Gentium*'.

Further development of an ecclesiology of communion

The Church of God is essentially a communion of persons incorporated into the Holy Trinity through Christ's flesh, which communicates eternal life to humanity. Now that we are more conscious of the 'theo-logical' character of the Council's ecclesiology, we can point to a few perspectives for deepening our understanding of the Church's sacramentality.

1 The common and hierarchical priesthoods

We need to come to a deeper understanding of this Trinitarian presence and action in the Church, in order to better appreciate the beauty of the relations and missionary dynamism that together constitute her being. The divine communion of persons in some sense prolongs itself in the communion of persons, functions and states of life in the Church. This is how the communion between pastors and the faithful expresses the communion between the Father and the Son. Baptism confers the grace of adoptive divine filiation, which points to the 'paternal' grace of the hierarchical priesthood: 'The tradition which sees the Bishop as an image of God the Father is quite ancient. As Saint Ignatius of Antioch wrote, the Father is like an invisible Bishop, the Bishop of all. Every Bishop, therefore, stands in the place of the Father of Jesus Christ in such a way that, precisely because of this representation, he is to be revered by all.'[14]

Exchanges of gifts take place within the People of God that in some way make visible the fruitful exchanges of the Trinity. This is why wherever communion between pastors and the faithful, between the hierarchical priesthood and the common priesthood of the baptized, is a living reality, we witness the flourishing of charisms of the Holy Spirit, religious and priestly vocations, and countless charitable and missionary initiatives. The Church's life thus shows itself to be a Trinitarian life that spreads through the world by means of a joyful and gratuitous missionary expansion.

The sacramentality of the Church is located precisely in the witnesses of paternity, filiation, fraternity and spiritual fruitfulness that make the ecclesial community fulfilling for its own members and attractive to the world. Most of

---

[14] John Paul II, Post-Synodal Apostolic Exhortation, *Pastoris Gregis*, 7. Cf. Ignatius of Antioch, Letter to the Magnesians, 6, 1; to the Trallians, 3; and to the Smyrneaens, 8, 1.

the time, from the outside, no one knows of the treasure buried in the field of the Church. This treasure is the fruitfulness of the divine persons who give themselves through the sacramental celebrations of baptism and the Eucharist, thus nourishing the fraternal life and the invincible joy of Christians. 'See how they love one another,'[15] exclaimed the pagans observing the life of the first Christian communities, whose members were capable of witnessing to the risen Christ to the point of martyrdom. The first challenge of Christian communities is to allow this joy at salvation to shine through them. Such joy springs from an authentic love of all, especially the poorest.

2 The universal Church and the particular churches

Among the questions that caught the attention of theologians after the Council and call for further development is the relation between the universal Church and the particular churches. One aspect of this is the communion of bishops with the Bishop of Rome, the successor of Peter and the head of the apostolic college. Here we need to avoid two pitfalls. The first involves a juridical, pyramid-like conception of the universal Church, which makes the particular churches and diocesan bishops executors of a central power. The second is a conception of the local church as self-sufficient, such that the universal Church is understood as a federation of diocesan communities that agree to mutual recognition. The Council's ecclesiology is much richer and more profound than these distortions, which reveal a theologically insufficient understanding of communion.

Let us begin with the notion of the diocese or particular church presented in the conciliar Decree *Christus Dominus*[16]:

> A diocese is a portion of the people of God which is entrusted to a bishop to be shepherded by him with the cooperation of the clergy. Thus by adhering to its pastor and gathered together by him through the Gospel and the Eucharist in the Holy Spirit, it constitutes a particular church in which the one, holy, catholic, and apostolic Church of Christ is truly present and operative. (*CD* 11)

The particular church is rightly valued if we consider it as a 'portion' of the universal Church, and not only as a part or a geographical region. 'Portion'

---

[15] Tertullian, *Apology*, 39, 7.
[16] Vatican Council II, Decree Concerning the Pastoral Office of Bishops *Christus Dominus*.

means that the universal Church is present in this portion and is the foundation for its communion with all the other portions. Together, they form a single Church. This presence of the one Church in each portion implies a relation of communion between the bishops, since they belong to the same apostolic college, over which the successor of Peter presides. For each bishop, this means full episcopal authority over the portion he has been given to shepherd, and whose communion with the universal Church he must ensure.

Since the modern-day Pentecost of Vatican Council II is in continuity with the first Pentecost in Jerusalem, today we see the universal Church spread throughout the world. But the Church's catholicity was already present as a seed in the Cenacle. This qualitative catholicity of the first Apostles gathered together with Mary in prayer continues to exist in each particular church, which forms a single subject with the Church of the origins.

Hence we cannot dream of another, purely spiritual or merely national Church, which would subordinate the Catholic truth to the imperatives of a given culture. The particular churches of Australia and Oceania are geographically situated at the opposite end of the earth from Rome. But each of these is a 'portion' of the universal Church. That is to say, each of these is a concrete realization of the Catholic Church and not a geographical department of a global collectivity.

The universal Church is one, holy, catholic and apostolic. All these properties are present here, since the Church's universal dimension is her divine dimension. That is to say, her universal dimension is the communion of the Trinity poured out in her through faith, baptism, the Eucharist and all the sacraments. The latter presuppose a living bond with all the other particular Catholic churches – in the first place, the Church of Rome, whose bishop 'presides in love'[17] over all the churches as the supreme pastor of the universal Church.

The Church of Christ, at once universal and particular, acts in the world as the bride of the incarnate Word, who invites all to participate in his mysteries. The Church communicates the life of the Trinity to the world through her

---

[17] Ignatius of Antioch, *Letter to the Romans*, Prologue: 'Ignatius … to the Church … which also presides in the chief place of the Roman territory; a church worthy of God, worthy of honor, worthy of felicitation, worthy of praise, worthy of success, worthy of sanctification, and presiding in love, maintaining the law of Christ, and bearer of the Father's name …' *The Epistles of St. Clement of Rome and St. Ignatius of Antioch* (trans. James A. Kleist, Ancient Christian Writers, vol. 1, New York/ Mahwah: Paulist Press, 1946), p. 80.

multiple relations of communion and mission: the communion of Christian spouses that is the basis of the domestic Church; the communion between a bishop, his priests and his people; the communion between the successor of Peter and the College of Bishops; the real but imperfect communion between churches and ecclesial communities; and communion in hope with the heavenly Church and the rest of humanity. This is how the Church is, in Christ, the universal sacrament of salvation, tending towards the eschatological fulfilment of history.

3 Unity in diversity

All our reflection on the ecclesiology of communion in the light of an explicitly Trinitarian discourse about God must lead to a mentality and attitudes that are coherent with and conformed to the Church's sacramental mission.

The Trinitarian foundation we highlighted presupposes unity in difference in God himself: 'One Love, three Lovers.' We are thus invited to cultivate unity in diversity in the Church's life and mission: the unity of love in the multiplicity of persons, the unity of faith and mores in the diversity of cultural and social contexts. Against every tendency to an ideological uniformity, ecclesial communities are called to recognize and protect the dignity of every person as a treasure, whatever his limits and faults. These communities must also value the bonds of communion founded on diverse functions and charisms, as well as on the different states of life that enrich one another as they incarnate the complementary 'faces' of holiness.

This spirit of unity in diversity encourages a great freedom in the organization of communities, methods of evangelization and forms of prayer. It recommends an attitude of continual dialogue in efforts to evangelize cultures and enculturate the Gospel. Love of unity also requires freedom of speech in the exercise of episcopal collegiality, so that decisions that have ripened in communion can be put into effect in a climate of shared responsibility. This love must also inspire attitudes of openness and patience in ecumenical and interreligious dialogue, or in all situations in which conflict threatens peace. For in all things, charity remains the key to unity in diversity.

In brief, the Church is the universal sacrament of salvation through all her forms of communion and mission, which bear witness to the communion of the Trinity at work in history. The Church must, then, appreciate diversity as a richness of unity, in the manner of the God who is one as three. 'That they may all be one; even as you, Father, are in me, and I in you, that they also may be in us, so that the world may believe that you have sent me' (Jn 17.21).

Conclusion

At the end of our investigation of the profound meaning of Vatican II's ecclesiology, we see that the *koinonia-communio* of the Spirit of the Father and the incarnate Son is, as it were, the Council's master key, as the principle of communion and mission. This key gives access to the mystery of the Church, the universal sacrament of salvation, in all its dimensions: Trinitarian, Christological, anthropological, ecumenical and pastoral.

From this flows a new image of the Church; the essentially missionary People of God animated by the Spirit of holiness. This Spirit is the Spirit of universal fraternity and of unity in diversity. All the members of God's people, laity, religious, priests and bishops, form a sacramental community, the body and bride of Christ. Through him, with him and in him, she shares in his unique priesthood, for the glory of God and the salvation of the world.

The Church's sacramental witness is at heart the witness of the Trinity in history: this is the essential core of the Council's ecclesiology. Such witness includes the Church's openness to the modern world and an attitude of dialogue with respect to it; it includes above all the Church's openness to all humanity through the proclamation of the Gospel, the promotion of religious freedom and peace, and ecumenical and interreligious dialogue. This missionary spirit emanates from the conciliar texts. It prompts various experiences of collegiality and integrates the various charisms the Spirit has given into the Church, so that she can evangelize today's world with courage and enthusiasm.

The Holy Spirit amply provided for the needs of the Church in our time. On the level of doctrine, the Council exceeded all expectations and predictions. On the pastoral level, it still challenges us to put its unrecognized or forgotten riches into practice. This is why Vatican Council II remains a grace to be received today.

3

A Council for the Laity? The Vision of Vatican II in Empowering the Lay Faithful

Anne Hunt

Introduction

The 1917 Code of Canon Law had only two general canons on the laity (c. 682, 683). It made a clear demarcation between the clergy and the laity (c. 107). The clergy always have precedence over the laity (c. 119). The laity cannot perform any act of jurisdiction or order (c. 948). The Code reflects the ecclesiology of the post-Tridentine Church, famously expressed by Pope Pius X who, in 1906, described the Church as essentially an *unequal* society.[1] That ecclesiology assumes a pyramidal model of church. The apostolate of the Church is basically that of the hierarchy.[2] Ministries pertain to the ordained. Custodianship of revelation resides with the hierarchy. Lay people effectively have the status of dependent children: it is for them to submit to and receive from the hierarchy. The theology of the Church's mission was also limited, with the work of evangelization considered to be that of missionaries and basically directed outside the Church. The laity, it seemed, had no mission. While necessarily reflecting the ecclesiological and historical circumstances of its era, it was nevertheless a deficient ecclesiology in a number of ways. Even the language used to describe the unordained faithful remained undeveloped with the term 'lay' in common parlance connoting the inexpert and unqualified in

---

[1] Pope Pius X, Encyclical, *Vehementer Nos* (1906), p. 8. http://www.vatican.va/holy_father/pius_x/encyclicals/documents/hf_p-x_enc_11021906_vehementer-nos_en.html.

[2] Pius XI wrote, for example, 'Catholic Action has no other purpose than the participation of the laity in the apostolate of the hierarchy.' Letter of Pius XI to Cardinal Bertam (13 November 1928), in Odile M. Liebard (ed.), *Clergy and Laity: Official Catholic Teachings* (Wilmington: McGrath, 1978), pp. 30–34 (31).

contrast to those with professional competence and authority, and as such was inadequate to the ecclesial reality of the laity.[3]

Movements of biblical, liturgical and ecumenical renewal in the decades leading up to Vatican II, together with a new awakening of the laity in apostolic action, particularly in the work of Catholic Action, and such movements as Young Christian Workers, Pax Romana and the Legion of Mary, provided strong impetus for the Council's consideration of the role of the laity. Pius X's Motu Proprio, *Tra le Sollicitudini, On Sacred Music* (1903), Pius XI's Apostolic Constitution, *Divini Cultus Sanctitatem, On Divine Worship* (1928) and Pius XII's encyclical *Mediator Dei, On the Sacred Liturgy* (1947) had meanwhile urged their active participation in the liturgy. These developments, as well as such influential studies as Yves Congar's *Jalons pour unethéologie de laïcat* (1953),[4] and Gérard Philips' *Le Rôle Du Laicat Dans L'Eglise* (1954) and *Pour une Christianisme adulte* (1962),[5] afforded rich resources for the Council's deliberations on questions concerning the laity. In what would constitute one of its major achievements, Vatican II would describe the lay faithful in positive terms, not as subordinates and non-clerics, but as members of the People of God sharing equally, by virtue of their baptism, in the salvific mission of the Church.

Vatican II's new ecclesial self-understanding and its vision of the laity in the Church

In contrast to the scant treatment of the laity in pre-Vatican II conciliar teachings, and reflecting a transition of immense proportions and complexity, almost every Vatican II document has something to say on the laity. As Avery Dulles observed, 'At the council the Catholic Church for the first time in history took up in its full scope the question of the status and role of the laity. If Vatican II had done nothing else, that fact alone would

---

3   See Karl Rahner, 'Notes on the Lay Apostolate', *Theological Investigations* (trans. Kark-H. Kruger; vol. 2; London: Darton, Longman and Todd, 1963), pp. 319–52; Edward Schillebeeckx, 'A New Type of Layman', in *The Mission of the Church* (trans. N. D. Smith; New York: Seabury, 1973), pp. 117–31 (125).

4   English translation, *Lay People in the Church: A Study for a Theology of Laity* (trans. Donald Attwater; London: Bloomsbury, 1957).

5   English translations, *The Role of the Laity in the Church* (trans. John R. Gilbert and James W. Moudry; Cork: Mercer, 1955) and *Achieving Christian Maturity* (trans. Eileen Kane; Dublin/Melbourne: Gill, 1966).

make the council historic.'[6] Admittedly, the Council's primary focus is the lay apostolate, as distinct from a theology of the lay state as such,[7] and there are apparent inconsistencies and juxtapositions in its statements,[8] but it was nevertheless a momentous development.

Sacrosanctum Concilium, the first of the documents to be debated and subsequently passed almost without emendation on 22 November 1963, signalled the Council's movement to a new ecclesial self-understanding. The constitution recognizes that the Church's nature and mission is derived from the will of the Triune God who wishes all to be saved (*SC* 5).[9] The liturgy is 'the chief means through which believers are expressing in their lives and demonstrating to others the mystery which is Christ, and *the sort of entity the true church really is*' (*SC* 2).[10] The theological and ecclesiological implications of this emerging ecclesial self-understanding were profound. As Massimo Faggioli has commented, *Sacrosanctum Concilium* 'gave voice to the call for church reform more generally'; and it 'constitutes one of the pillars of the ecclesiology of Vatican II.'[11] Its ramifications for the Council's teaching on the laity in particular were to reverberate through the conciliar documents.

In what amounted to a very significant development in thinking about the identity and role of the laity, in *Sacrosanctum Concilium* the Council famously declares: 'The church very much wants all believers [*fideles*] to be led to take a full, conscious and active part in liturgical celebration. This is demanded by the nature of the liturgy itself; and, by virtue of their baptism, it is the

---

[6] Avery Dulles, 'Can the Word "Laity" Be Defined?' *Origins* 18.29 (29 December 1988), p. 471.

[7] Jan Grootaers writes: 'One of the thorniest issues in the discussion was once again how to lay hold of so fluid a concept as "lay person" and how to succeed in defining it. Neither canon law nor attempts to derive a theological concept satisfied the Commission, which had to be content with a pragmatic approach and a simple description.' Jan Grootaers, 'The Drama Continues Between the Acts: The "Second Preparation" and its Opponents', in Giuseppe Alberigo (ed.), *History of Vatican II* (English edn, ed. Joseph A. Komonchak; vol. 2; Maryknoll, NY: Orbis; Leuven: Peeters, 2003), p. 407.

[8] As Hermann Pottmeyer has noted: 'But even juxtaposition is progress, because by being complemented the older thesis is relativised as one-sided and bearings are given for further development in understanding of the faith. The needed synthesis is a task the Council sets for the Church and for theologians; it is a task of reception, which is far from being a merely passive process.' 'A New Phase in the Reception of Vatican II: Twenty Years of Interpretation of the Council', in Giuseppe Alberigo, Jean-Pierre Jossua and Joseph A. Komonchak (eds.), *The Reception of Vatican II* (trans. Matthew J. O'Connell; Tunbridge Wells: Burns & Oats, 1987), pp. 27–43 (38).

[9] See Anne Hunt, 'The Trinitarian Depths of Vatican II', *Theological Studies* 74 (2013), pp. 3–19.

[10] Emphases added. All English translations of Vatican II texts are taken from *Decrees of the Ecumenical Councils* (ed. Norman P. Tanner; Washington: Georgetown University, 1990).

[11] Massimo Faggioli, '*Sacrosanctum Concilium* and the Meaning of Vatican II', *Theological Studies* 71 (2010), pp. 437–52 (450). The question remains open, however, as to what ecclesiology Eucharistic, *communio*, trinitarian, paschal, etc – might be described as *the* ecclesiology of the Council.

right and duty of the Christian people' (*SC* 14).[12] The laity were not to be merely passive recipients or docile observers of liturgical rites performed by the clergy. Their participation in the liturgy was to be full, conscious and active, this as their right and duty, by virtue of their baptism. It is this radical retrieval of the significance of baptism and this imperative for the laity's full and active participation that was to extend to the life and mission of the Church that would subsequently resound through the conciliar teachings, although not without evident tension at times with theological and pastoral understandings of the pre-conciliar Church.

The ramifications of this new ecclesial self-understanding and its associated revisioning of the identity and role, and rights and duties of the laity are most clearly seen in the Constitution *Lumen Gentium*. The Council Fathers had rejected the preparatory schema, *De Ecclesia*, and insisted on a very different treatment of the subject.[13] *Lumen Gentium* was indeed a very different document and it is remarkable in so many ways. First, in starting with the words, *Lumen Gentium*, Light of the Nations, it proclaims that it is Christ who is Light of the world. An ecclesiocentrism is thus implicitly disallowed, triumphalist notions set aside and Church structures relativized: the Church is not itself the Light but is there to serve the Light. The later conciliar decree, *Ad Gentes*, in another development of tremendous significance for the Council's new ecclesial self-understanding, describes the nature of the Church as fundamentally missionary, springing from the Trinitarian mystery of God and the missions of the Son and Spirit and, furthermore, that the Church's missionary activity pertains not only to missionaries, but to all the faithful by virtue of their participation through baptism in the very life of the Trinity (*AG* 6). Secondly, and of profound significance, *Lumen Gentium* proceeds to a reflection on the Church as mystery, not as perfect society or hierarchical constitution, but mystery grounded in the mystery of the Trinity (*LG* 2–4; *GS* 40).[14] Again, *Lumen Gentium* implicitly

---

[12] For precursors in the liturgical movement to this conciliar teaching, see Jozef Lamberts, 'L'évolution de la notion de "participation active" dans le Mouvement liturgique du Vingtième siècle', *La Maison-Dieu* 241 (2005), pp. 77–120.

[13] Archbishop of Melbourne, Daniel Mannix, was scathing in his criticism of it, specifically criticizing, among other things, its teachings on the laity. See Jeffrey J. Murphy, 'The Lost (and Last) Animadversions of Daniel Mannix', *Australasian Catholic Record* 76 (1999), pp. 54–73 (70).

[14] Giuseppi Alberigo notes: 'Vatican II repeatedly highlighted the mystery-dimension of the Christian message. *Mystery* is used here in the charged and biblical sense of the word.' 'Transition to a New Age', in Giuseppe Alberigo (ed.), *History of Vatican II* (English edn, ed. Joseph A. Komonchak; trans. Matthew J. O'Connell; vol. 5; Maryknoll: Orbis, Leuven: Peeters, 2006), p. 629.

relativizes the hierarchical structure of the Church vis-à-vis the Church's mission. Thirdly, the constitution then proceeds, before any consideration of structure and jurisdiction, roles, rights and responsibilities, or indeed of membership as such, to speak in richly biblical terms of the Church as mystery lived out historically as the People of God.[15] The council teaches that 'though they differ in essence and not simply in degree', the common priesthood of the faithful and the ministerial priesthood share in the one priesthood of Christ (*LG* 10). Here, in this understanding of the Church as the People of God, with all sharing in the three offices of Christ (the teaching office, the sanctifying office, the governing office) and in responsibility for the mission of the Church by virtue of their baptism is another of the pillars of the ecclesiology of Vatican II.[16]

Only after treating the Church as mystery lived out as the People of God does *Lumen Gentium* proceed to treat the hierarchical constitution of the Church. What is first asserted, to be clearly reiterated on numerous occasions, is the basic equality, dignity and call to discipleship that is fundamentally grounded in baptism and thus common to all the faithful as such. As stated in the new Code of Canon Law (1983), revised in the light of the Council,[17] 'From their rebirth in Christ, there exists among all the Christian faithful a true equality regarding dignity and action by which they all cooperate in the building up of the Body of Christ according to each one's own condition and function' (c. 208).[18] The pre-conciliar characterization of the laity as 'not cleric or religious' is set aside and replaced by a positive characterization in terms of all the baptized sharing in the salvific mission of the Church. The Church is not a pyramid of unequals.[19] All of the faithful are made 'one in fellowship

---

[15] Joseph Komonckak writes: 'After noting that "people of God" here meant the whole body of the faithful, clergy and laity alike, it was explained that the new chapter *continued the consideration of the intimate nature, or mystery, of the Church* begun in the first chapter and that it had been made a separate chapter simply because a single chapter would be too large.' Joseph Komonchak, 'Toward an Ecclesiology of Communion', in Giuseppe Alberigo (ed.), *History of Vatican II* (English edn, ed. Joseph A. Komonchak; vol. 4; Maryknoll, NY: Orbis; Leuven: Peeters, 2003), pp. 43–44. Emphasis added.

[16] For a discussion of 'priesthood' and 'the three offices' as overarching categories in *Lumen Gentium*, see Orm Rush, 'The Offices of Christ, *Lumen Gentium* and the People's Sense of the Faith', *Pacifica* 16 (2003), pp. 137–52.

[17] In promulgating the revised Code, John Paul II stressed that the Council was the 'essential point of reference' for interpretation of the Code. John Paul II, Apostolic Constitution, *Sacrae Disciplinae Leges* (25 January 1983), http://www.vatican.va/holy_father/john_paul_ii/apost_constitutions/documents/hf_jp-ii_apc_25011983_sacrae-disciplinae-leges_en.html.

[18] Code of Canon Law (1983), http://www.vatican.va/archive/ENG1104/__PU.HTM.

[19] Yves Congar writes: 'The church receives the fullness of the Spirit only in the totality of the gifts made by all her members. She is a not pyramid whose passive base receives everything from the apex.' 'Pneumatology Today', *American Ecclesiastical Review* 167 (1973), pp. 435–49 (443).

and ministry' by the Spirit (*LG* 4), all 'of every rank' are gifted by the Holy Spirit (*LG* 12) and all share in the Church's mission (*LG* 5). In underscoring an understanding of the Church as a community of radical equality, by virtue of a common baptism, it is not however a democratic notion that is intended or implied, but rather a vision of Church as a dynamic *communio*, based on the analogy with the mystery of the Trinity; and herein is another of the pillars of the ecclesiology of Vatican II.[20]

The Council's recognition of the Church as mystery, grounded in the Trinity, and lived out historically in the People of God, leads to the retrieval of the notion of the *sensus fidei*, that instinct for the faith and that sharing in discernment of the faith that resides in the whole People of God.[21] As *Lumen Gentium* explains:

> The universal body of the faithful who have received the anointing of the holy one, cannot be mistaken in belief [*in credendo falli nequit*]. It displays this particular property through a supernatural sense of the faith in the whole people when 'from the bishops to the last of the faithful laity' it expresses the consent of all in matters of faith and morals. (*LG* 12)

Similarly, *Dei Verbum* teaches that the Holy Spirit enlightens all the faithful (*DV* 8), and that, with the help of the Holy Spirit, there is 'growth in understanding of what is handed on' and that thus 'the church constantly holds its course towards the fullness of God's truth' (*DV* 8).[22] Vatican II thus recognizes that all the faithful have a right, authority and responsibility to preserve and penetrate the faith.[23] It calls for collaboration and co-responsibility in discerning and articulating the meaning of

---

[20] According to Ladislas Orsy: '*Communio* was the central theme of the Council. ... The Council Fathers made a profession of faith in the church of Christ as the *communio* of believers. ... The Council lifted up the church to a new vision, or into a new field of vision.' Orsy adds that the Council, however, 'left little guidance for its implementation.' Ladislas Orsy, *Receiving the Council: Theological and Canonical Insights and Debates* (Collegeville, MN: Liturgical, 2009), p. xiii.

[21] For consideration of the sense of faith, the sensus and consensus of the faithful, see Francis A. Sullivan, 'The Sense of Faith: The Sense/Consensus of the Faithful', in Bernard Hoose (ed.), *Authority in the Roman Catholic Church: Theory and Practice* (Aldershot, Hants: Ashgate, 2002), pp. 85–93. See also the careful study by Daniel J. Finucane, *Sensus Fidelium: The Use of a Concept in the Post-Vatican II Era* (San Francisco: International Scholars Publications, 1996).

[22] On the issues of renewal and reform, see Peter De Mey, 'Church Renewal and Reform in the Documents of Vatican II: History, Theology, Terminology', *The Jurist* 71 (2011), pp. 369–400.

[23] Orm Rush writes: 'The manner of that participation [of all believers in the office of teaching] and the active role of the *sensus fidelium* in formal exercise of the teaching office by the magisterium is one of the burning issues in the ongoing reception of Vatican II.' 'The Offices of Christ, *Lumen Gentium* and the People's Sense of the Faith', p. 150.

the Christian faith.[24] It cannot be assumed, then, that the lay faithful are necessarily misguided, ill-informed or recalcitrant when they disagree or are in conflict with the hierarchy on matters of faith and morals.[25]

Turning its attention to the hierarchical constitution of the Church, the Council teaches that the hierarchy is part of the People of God and that it exists for the service of the People of God (*LG* 18; see also *CD* 16). The episcopacy's task is to discern, judge and order the charisms of the Spirit (*LG* 12, 23–4; *AA* 3). The clergy have unique authority that comes from sacramental ordination (*LG* 21), while bishops enjoy the fullness of the sacrament of orders (*LG* 21) and are authentic teachers (*LG* 24). Vatican II also teaches, however, that the hierarchy are not solely or exclusively possessors of divine revelation. While they have responsibility for naming and defining doctrine, their articulation of it should reflect the faith of the community of the faithful (*LG* 37).

Specifically addressing issues concerning the laity in Chapter 4,[26] the Council first stresses that 'everything that was said about the People of God applies equally to the laity, religious and clerics' (*LG* 30). The Council Fathers acknowledge the contribution of the laity to the Church and their co-responsibility for the mission: 'The sacred pastors are well aware of how much the laity contribute to the well-being of the whole Church. They know that they were not instituted by Christ to undertake by themselves alone the church's whole mission of salvation of the world' (*LG* 30).

The constitution adopts a fairly pragmatic working definition of the laity:

> Under the title of laity are here understood to mean all Christ's faithful [*christifideles*], except those who are in sacred orders or are members of a religious state that is recognised by the church; that is to say, the faithful [*christifideles*] who, since they have been incorporated into Christ by baptism, constitute the people of God and, in their own way made sharers in Christ's priestly, prophetic, and royal office, play their own part in the mission of the whole christian people in the church and in the world. (*LG* 31)

---

[24] Cardinal Suenens, in *Coresponsibility in the Church* (New York: Herder and Herder, 1968), p. 28, described co-responsibility as 'the central idea of Vatican II.'

[25] For treatment of the presence of conflict and the absence of the sense of the faithful, see Daniel J. Finucane, *Sensus Fidelium: The Use of a Concept in the Post-Vatican II Era*, pp. 238–39.

[26] Joseph Komonchak notes that this chapter 'was the least controversial of all the chapters in the schema.' 'Toward an Ecclesiology of Communion', p. 45.

Again, the Council stresses the identity of the Church as the People of God who, in and through baptism, share in the threefold office – priestly, prophetic and royal – of Christ and thus in the mission of the Church, both 'in the church and in the world.' Participation in Christ's threefold office is thus not delegated or deputed to the laity by the hierarchy, nor is it a sharing in the apostolate of the hierarchy. Rather, all the baptized – male and female, ordained and lay – share in Christ's *tria munera*, and thus in the mission of the Church. While not all participate in the Church's mission in the same way, no one is excluded or exempt from the baptismal call to share in it. The Council stresses: 'There is, therefore, no inequality in Christ and in the church, with regard to race or nation, social condition or sex, … there is a true equality of all with regard to the dignity and action common to all the faithful concerning the building up of the body of Christ' (*LG* 32). *Lumen Gentium* again affirms that Christ continues to carry out his prophetic task

> not only through the hierarchy who teach in his name and by his power, but also through the laity [*laicos*], whom [Christ] constitutes his witnesses and equips with an understanding of the faith [*sensus fidei*] and a grace of speech precisely so that the power of the gospel may shine forth in the daily life of family and society. (*LG* 35)

The Council describes the distinctiveness of the laity in terms of 'their secular character' (*LG* 31), by which means the laity make the Gospel present and active in the world in a way that is distinct from that of the clergy. The Council's description of the distinctiveness of the laity in terms of 'their secular character' is more than a merely phenomenological or sociological comment. It is not simply their living in the world that constitutes their secular nature, but rather the *way* in which the laity make the Gospel present in the world which is distinct from the clergy. The laity are the Church active in the world. Indeed, they are to take the initiative in the transformation of the temporal order (*LG* 31; *GS* 43). This secular character is no accident, deficit or impediment but is positively constitutive of the apostolate of the laity.

While the Council describes the laity in terms of their apostolate in and for the world (*LG* 31; *AA* 2, 5, 7; see also *GS* 43), it does not however propose a hard and fast separation or division of apostolates, with the world as the arena of the laity and the Church as that of the ordained (see, e.g., *LG* 2, *AA* 9 and *GS* 43). While *Lumen Gentium* indicates a tendency to restrict the role of the laity to the world and not within the Church as such, the later conciliar document, *Gaudium et spes*, clearly acknowledges the secular as the arena of the whole Church (*GS* 40). The Council thus disallows a relegation of the laity's apostolate to the secular arena alone. The unordained may have roles within the Church, such as catechesis, liturgy, pastoral roles (*AA* 24), even administration (*AA* 5, 10) and indeed roles 'for a spiritual aim' (*LG* 33; see also *SC* 79), and the ordained have roles in the world (*LG* 31; see also *GS* 43). The building up of the Church and the fulfilment of its mission, in the Church and in the world, is the work of the whole community of believers, a co-responsibility.[27] The laity not only have the right but the responsibility to be actively involved in the Church's apostolate (*LG* 30, 33). Just as all share in the mission of the Church, similarly all are called to holiness. The council teaches that, while there are different kinds of life and different duties, 'there is one holiness cultivated by all who are led by the Spirit of God' (*LG* 41).

The Council has much to say about the relationship between the laity and ordained. *Lumen Gentium* teaches that:

> the laity, like all the faithful, should be prompt to accept in a spirit of christian obedience those decisions that the sacred pastors make as teachers and governors of the church and as representatives of Christ. ... Nor should they neglect to commend to God in their prayers those who have been placed over them, that they may do their work with joy and not sadly. (*LG* 37)

Perhaps nowhere does the Council speak more strongly of the role of the laity than in *LG* 37 where it teaches that the clergy are to help and support the laity in their apostolate and also to engage their skills and counsel:

> The sacred pastors are to acknowledge and promote the dignity and the responsibility of the laity in the church; they should willingly make use of their prudent counsel; they should confidently entrust to them offices in

---

[27] Pope John Paul II in his Apostolic Exhortation speaks of all the baptized as 'active and coresponsible' (§ 21). http://www.vatican.va/holy_father/john_paul_ii/apost_exhortations/documents/hf_jp-ii_exh_30121988_christifideles-laici_en.html. In a homily in 1998, John Paul II speaks of esteem for the laity for their 'great commitment to the *co-responsibility* which is theirs through Baptism and Confirmation' in enlivening parish communities (§ 4). Emphasis in the original. http://www.vatican.va/holy_father/john_paul_ii/homilies/1998/documents/hf_jp-ii_hom_19980619_austria-salzburg_en.html. Pope Benedict XVI, in a speech in May 2009, speaks of 'a renewed awareness of our being Church and of the pastoral co-responsibility which, in Christ's name, we are all called to exercise.' http://www.vatican.va/holy_father/benedict_xvi/speeches/2009/may/documents/hf_ben-xvi_spe_20090526_convegno-diocesi-rm_en.html.

the service of the church and leave them freedom and space to act. Indeed they should encourage them to take up work on their own initiative. With a father's love they should pay careful attention in Christ to the projects, the requests and the desires put forward by the laity. (*LG* 37)

While the reference to the pastor as father and, by implication, the laity as children, betrays the paternalism of pre-conciliar attitudes, the Council unambiguously expresses respect for the competence of the laity and indeed for the laity's rights as members of the faithful (*LG* 36–7).[28] Indeed, *Gaudium et spes* notes that the laity should not be looking to the clergy for answers to every concrete issue, nor thinking that this is the clergy's role (*GS* 43). The Council again speaks very strongly when it acknowledges that 'in accordance with the knowledge, competence or authority that they possess, they [the laity] have the right and indeed sometimes the duty to make known their opinions on matters which concern the good of the church' (*LG* 37). The council adds: 'If possible this should be done through the institutions set up for this purpose by the church; and it should always be done with respect for the truth, with courage and with prudence, and in a spirit of reverence and love towards those who by reason of their sacred office represent Christ' (*LG* 37).

The Decree on the Lay Apostolate, *Apostolicam Actuositatem*, while theologically less sophisticated and of lesser significance in the conciliar corpus than *Lumen Gentium*, is no less historic. Never before had the laity been the subject of a decree by an ecumenical council.[29] *Apostolicam Actuositatem* reiterates that lay people, sharing in the priestly, prophetic and kingly offices of Christ, have their part to play in the one mission of the whole People of God in the Church and in the world (*AA* 2; *LG* 31). It exhorts the laity: 'Let [laypeople] show themselves to be [Christ's] cooperators, in the various forms and ways of proceeding with the one apostolate of the church, always adapting themselves to the new needs of the hour' (*AA* 33).

---

[28] The 1983 Code of Canon Law speaks of the obligations and rights of the lay Christian faithful, as well as those of clerics. http://www.vatican.va/archive/ENG1104/_INDEX.HTM.

[29] Just as significantly, laypersons, including the Australian lay woman, Rosemary Goldie, were involved in the redaction of the conciliar texts. Jan Grootaers writes: 'Goldie's most important contribution to the Council in 1963 was the communication to the fathers of her panoramic view of the activity of the laity in the world.' 'The Drama Continues Between the Acts: The "Second Preparation" and its Opponents,' in *History of Vatican II*, vol. 2, p. 441 n. 194.

The Council acknowledges again that the apostolate of the laity derives from Christ himself, not from the hierarchy (*AA* 3), and that it is the work of the Holy Spirit, who gives charisms to the faithful[30]:

> Through receiving these gifts of grace, however unspectacular, everyone of the faithful has the right and duty to exercise them in the church and in the world for the good of humanity and the building up of the church. They do this in the freedom of the Spirit 'who blows where he wills' and, at the same time, in communion with the fellowship in Christ, especially with his pastors, whose part it is to judge about their true nature and ordered use, not indeed so as to extinguish the Spirit but in order to test everything and to hold on to what is good. (*AA* 3; see also *AA* 5, 9)

The laity exercise their apostolate both in the Church and in the world, in both the spiritual and the temporal orders (*AA* 5, 9). The apostolates of the laity and the clergy 'complement each other' (*AA* 6). The Council recognizes that 'within christian communities [the laity's] activity is so necessary that without it the pastors' apostolate cannot generally attain its full effect' (*AA* 10). The Council also urges the laity that 'they should not restrict their cooperation within the boundaries of their parish or diocese but rather be concerned to extend it to inter-parochial, inter-diocesan, national or international fields' (*AA* 10). The decree highlights the importance of education and formation of the laity (*AA* 26–32). In these ways, the Council expresses a vision of an educated and responsible laity engaged in the mission of the Church for the transformation of the world according to the values of the Kingdom of God, not simply at the behest of the hierarchy, but in communion with it, in response to a calling and commissioning by virtue of their lay state and their own expertise and charisms.

Responsibility is, however, to be balanced by accountability; autonomy by authority. The Council reminds all the faithful that 'union with those to whom the holy Spirit has given charge to rule the church of God is an essential element

---

[30] For Cardinal Suenens' influential speech to the Council in regard to charisms in the church, see 'The Charismatic Dimension of the Church', in Yves Congar, Hans Küng, and Daniel O'Hanlon (eds.), *Council Speeches of Vatican II* (London/New York: Sheed and Ward, 1964), pp. 18–21. John O'Malley notes that the concept of 'charism' was part of Vatican II's lexicon. 'Words like "charism", "dialogue", "partnership", "cooperation", and "friendship" indicate a new style for the exercise of authority and implicitly advocate a conversion to a new style of thinking, speaking, and behaving, a change from a more authoritarian and unidirectional style to a more reciprocal and responsible model.' *What Happened at Vatican II* (Cambridge, MA: Belknap of Harvard, 2008), p. 11.

of the christian apostolate' and that 'no less necessary is cooperation, suitably ordered by the hierarchy, between different initiatives in the apostolate' (*AA* 23). As well as 'appropriate coordination,' there should be 'charity of fellowship' and 'mutual esteem' among all forms of apostolate in the Church. 'Harmful competition' between different initiatives of the apostolate is to be avoided (*AA* 23). *Apostolicam Actuositatem* is noteworthy in the conciliar corpus for its acknowledgement of women's full participation in the apostolate of the laity, their role not limited to that of wife and mother: 'Since women are increasingly taking an active part in the whole life of society, it is important that their participation in the various fields of the church's apostolate should also increase' (*AA* 9).[31]

In its constitution treating the Church in the modern world (*GS*),[32] the Council's vision for the role of the laity in the life and mission of the Church is more implicit than explicit. *Gaudium et spes* makes only six explicit references to lay persons, and the first of them not until *GS* 43. In contrast to *Lumen Gentium*, *Gaudium et spes* emphasizes the secular character of the mission of the *whole* Church and the apostolate to the world as the responsibility of the *entire* Church (*GS* 40). It acknowledges the clergy's limited competence in the secular arena and urges the laity to take up its own distinctive role:

> The laity may expect enlightenment and spiritual help from the clergy. But they should not consider that their pastors always have the expertise needed to provide a concrete and ready answer to every problem which arises, even the most serious ones, or that this is their mission. The laity, as enlightened with Christian wisdom and paying careful attention to the teaching of the magisterium, have their own part to play. (*GS* 43)

Gaudium et spes thus acknowledges a certain autonomy to the exercise of the laity's mission and ministry.[33] It reiterates the co-responsibility of the faithful for the Church's mission, while also stressing the specialist expertise of clergy and theologians (*GS* 44). Moreover, it encourages the laity to study theology and scripture and, indeed, to contribute to the development of the sacred sciences (*GS* 62).

---

[31] *Gaudium et spes* also acknowledges women: 'Women are now at work in almost every sphere of life, and it is fitting that they should be able to play their full part according to their disposition' (*GS* 60).

[32] Alberigo comments that *Gaudium et spes* 'complete[s] the conciliar revolution.' Giuseppe Alberigo, 'Transition to a New Age', p. 635.

[33] Avery Cardinal Dulles notes that 'the Council applied the word "ministry" only rarely to lay persons, but those instances, though few in number, are significant in view of later developments.' 'The Mission of the Laity', L. J. McGinley Lecture, Fordham University (29 March 2006), http://old.usccb.org/laity/laymin/CardinalDulles.pdf.

Opportunities and challenges for lay participation in the Church

This, in necessarily brief outline, is Vatican II's grand vision for the role of the laity in the Church, born of the Council's new ecclesial self-understanding and its retrieval of the radical theology of baptism of the early Christian communities.[34] Fifty years after Vatican II, much has been achieved. The Catholic laity includes increasing numbers of well-educated – including theologically well-educated – competent men and women. Catholic laity are to be found in significant positions of administration and governance in Church agencies, some of them multi-million dollar enterprises, some multinational enterprises. Indeed, with the rapid decline in the numbers of clergy and religious in that same period, the administration and delivery of Catholic education, healthcare and social welfare agencies, at least in the West, is now very largely in the hands of lay people. The shift in lay participation in and leadership of Church agencies at the parish, diocesan, national and international levels has been momentous.

There is, however, more of Vatican II's vision that is yet to be achieved. Despite their involvement in and leadership of church agencies, the laity have little influence and involvement in the decision-making and governance of the Church as such, as distinct from its agencies in which they are employed. In this respect, co-responsibility has not yet taken root. Consider, for example, the lack of consultation in the decision to bring clergy from other countries to deal with the dwindling number of parish priests and in the various other strategies implemented to meet the pastoral needs of parish communities. Consider the appointments of parish priests to parishes and to the episcopacy without consultation with the laity. In that domain of Church life, there is often little consultation with the laity, even though these decisions impact directly on the laity and the life of the local church. If and when members of the laity are consulted, it is often only in regard to financial and administration matters, as if these are the only areas of non-ordained expertise. If and when they are invited to participate in parish councils or diocesan synods, their

---

[34] Evidence from the early Church indicates a much more radical theology of baptism, with the laity consulted in matters concerning the Church, particularly in relation to the selection of church leaders. See Paul Lakeland, *Catholicism at the Crossroads: How the Laity Can Save the Church* (New York: Continuum, 2007), p. 69. Also Cardinal Léon-Joseph Suenens, *Coresponsibility in the Church* (New York: Herder and Herder, 1968), p. 188.

views are but advisory. Ecclesiastical jurisdiction remains the prerogative of the ordained, without even the requirement to consult. Pope Francis himself recently raised this issue with the CELAM leadership:

> Is pastoral discernment a habitual criterion, through the use of Diocesan Councils? Do such Councils and Parish Councils, whether pastoral or financial, provide real opportunities for lay people to participate in pastoral consultation, organization and planning? The good functioning of these Councils is critical. I believe that on this score, we are far behind.[35]

Meanwhile, many of the laity stand aghast in the face of the scandals that have unfolded in the Church in recent years: corruption (Vatileaks), poor management and administration (Vatican Bank), and, most alarmingly of all, the sex abuse crisis, all of which have blighted the Church, and all of them indicative of poor governance. Many have left the Church out of a sense of disappointment and dismay. Those who remain have competencies and charisms to bring to Church decision-making, but little opportunity by which to place them at the disposal of the Church. Had the laity been consulted and engaged in decision-making in these areas, the issues which now undermine the credibility of the Church and its leaders may have been more appropriately addressed and the scandals averted. The significant roles and responsibilities which members of the laity now exercise in Church agencies provide strong grounds for hope, courage and confidence that we as a Church can further advance the implementation of the Council's vision.

Key areas for attention

Several areas for attention in enhancing lay participation in the Church are evident in the contemporary situation.

1 Consultation with the laity

The Church is necessarily structured and ordered for mission. The hierarchy's responsibility for governance does not, however, preclude consultation with the laity. Indeed, the People of God should be consulted in appropriate ways

---

[35] Pope Francis 1, http://en.radiovaticana.va/news/2013/07/29/pope_francis:_address_to_celam_leadership/in2-714915.

in matters that concern the good of the Church, its life and its mission, for, as the Council recognized, the laity, by virtue of their baptism, also have an active role to play in the Church's teaching, sanctifying and governing offices and its mission. Consultation should include not just administrative matters but extend to the three offices. It is not that the Church is a democracy, with decisions determined by opinion poll or majority vote, but neither is the Church a monarchy or oligarchy, with decisions handed down without appropriate consultation.

There is considerable room within the current canon law and Church teaching for meaningful consultation in decision-making, as distinct from decision-taking, which remains the responsibility of the hierarchy. As Vatican II stated in its *Decree on the Pastoral Office of Bishops in the Church*:

> The fathers of the council judge that it would be of great service for these departments [of the curia] to hear more often the views of lay people distinguished for their virtue, knowledge and experience in order that they too may play an appropriate part in the affairs of the church. (*CD* 10)

The challenge is to move to a more appropriate balance between the Church's hierarchical constitution and the cooperation and collaboration of the faithful as a whole by instituting structures, processes and policies for consultation with the laity, so that consultation becomes the order of the day, the modus operandi, the rule not the exception. The move would also serve the goal of achieving the high standards of accountability, transparency, subsidiarity and respect for proper process that characterize good governance.

2 Facilitating the participation of the laity

Many among the lay faithful have extensive experience and expertise in the professional areas of administration and governance, as well as other talents and training to bring to the Church. The Council urges church leaders at all levels to 'make use of their prudent counsel' (*LG* 37).[36] Pope Francis has also specifically challenged church leaders in this regard:

---

[36] When Blessed John Henry Newman urged consultation with the laity, he wrote: 'If our words or tone were disrespectful in thinking, we deeply grieve and apologise for such a fault; but surely we are not disrespectful in thinking, and in having thought, that the Bishop would like to know the sentiments of an influential portion of the laity before they took any step which perhaps they could not recall.' Editorial note by Newman, in *The Rambler* (May 1859), quoted in 'Introduction', in *On Consulting the Faithful in Matters of Doctrine* (ed. with an introduction by John Coulson; London: Geoffrey Chapman, 1961), p. 13. It is a question of prudent counsel in order to avoid a decision that lacks prudence.

> As pastors, bishops and priests, are we conscious and convinced of the mission of the lay faithful and do we give them the freedom to continue discerning, in a way befitting their growth as disciples, the mission which the Lord has entrusted to them? Do we support them and accompany them, overcoming the temptation to manipulate them or infantilize them? Are we constantly open to letting ourselves be challenged in our efforts to advance the good of the Church and her mission in the world?[37]

Again, we as Church are urged to develop and implement structures, processes and policies which call forth and facilitate the participation of the laity in the mission of the Church and the discernment of the *sensus fidelium* as envisaged by Vatican II. As Stephen Bevans suggests, it is for the ordained ministry to call forth the ministry of the Church. Ordained ministers are not 'to do it all,' but to inspire, discern, see to the training of, regulate, admonish and console the variety of ministries so that the Church, well equipped for ministry, can faithfully witness to the reign of God in the world. The ministry of bishops and priests is specifically to call forth the ministry of the whole Church, so that the Church can do mission and it is the priest who is most closely placed, in the name of the bishop, for calling forth the church's ministry, and so inspire people to participate in God's mission in the world.[38]

The Council also encouraged the education and formation of the laity for their roles in the Church at all levels – parish, diocese and catholic agencies – and in particular stressed their theological education. The Church is now better resourced than ever with considerable numbers of theologically well-educated lay people who could be appropriately involved in decision-making concerning the good of the Church and its mission. Vatican II recognized that the Church is ever in process, developing and maturing, and never fully possessing or understanding her own nature and mission (*LG* 5). *Gaudium et spes* underscores the responsibility of the *whole* Church for the Church's progress on her pilgrim way:

> It is for God's people as a whole, with the help of the holy Spirit, and especially for pastors and theologians, to listen to the various voices of

---

[37] Pope Francis' address to CELAM, http://en.radiovaticana.va/news/2013/07/29/pope_francis:_address_to_celam_leadership/in2-714915.

[38] Stephen Bevans, 'The Mission Has a Church, the Mission Has Ministers: Thinking Missiologically about Ministry and the Shortage of Priests', *Compass: A Review of Topical Theology* 43.3 (2009), p. 3.

our day, discerning them and interpreting them, and to evaluate them in the light of the divine word, so that revealed truth can be increasingly appropriated, better understood and more suitably expressed. (*GS* 44)

As Pope John XXIII explained in his address at the opening of the Council: 'For the deposit of faith, the truths contained in our venerable doctrine, are one thing; the fashion in which they are expressed, but with the same meaning and the same judgement, is another thing.'[39]

3 Tackling clericalism

Part of the challenge facing the Church is tackling a culture of clericalism and careerism in the Church. The Council's teachings and vision disallow clericalism and careerism any part in the exercise of the ordained ministry. Nor are the faithful to succumb to a quasi-clericalism in the exercise of their ministries. 'Careerism is leprosy', Pope Francis has warned.[40] But cultural change is no easy task; the challenge of changing a deep-rooted culture is enormous. We as Church, ordained and laity, need to address this serious issue together. Pertinent here too is the role of women in the Church. Their marginalization in the decision-making and governance of the Church is not only indefensible in light of the Council's teachings regarding the fundamental equality, dignity and vocation to holiness of all, but it is also a contributing factor in the culture of clericalism. Consultation with and the active involvement of the laity, both women and

[39] Pope John XXIII, *Acta apostolicae sedis* 54 (1962), pp. 785–96 (791); ET, http://jakomonchak.files.wordpress.com/2012/10/john-xxiii-opening-speech.pdf.

[40] Pope Francis, http://en.radiovaticana.va/news/2013/06/06/pope_to_future_diplomats:_careerism_is_leprosy!/in2-699076. Pope Francis has spoken of the dangers of clericalism on several occasions in the first few months of his papacy. See http://en.radiovaticana.va/news/2013/04/18/do_not_be_afraid_to_go_out_%E2%80%98into_the_deep%E2%80%99,_pope_to_argentine_bishops/in2-684297; http://en.radiovaticana.va/news/2013/05/24/total_love_for_jesus_is_the_measure_of_a_man_of_god,_pope_tell/in2-695261; http://en.radiovaticana.va/news/2013/07/29/pope_francis:_address_to_celam_leadership/in2-714915. See also, for example, R. Kevin Seasoltz, 'Clericalism: A Sickness in the Church', *The Furrow: A Journal for the Contemporary Church* 61 (2010), pp. 135–42; Dean R. Hoge and Jacqueline E. Wenger, *Evolving Visions of the Priesthood: Changes from Vatican II to the Turn of the New Century* (Collegeville, MN: Liturgical Press, 2003). See also Archbishop Mark Coleridge's reflections on church culture as a systemic contributing factor in the sexual abuse crisis, in ABC Radio National, *Encounter*, 'Where is the Fire of Pentecost: Sexual Abuse, the Catholic Church and Culture' (23 May 2010), http://www.abc.net.au/radionational/programs/encounter/where-is-the-fire-of-pentecost-sexual-abuse-the/3043702. For an analysis of the child sexual abuse crisis, in reference to clerical identity and culture, see Marie Keenan, *Child Sexual Abuse and the Catholic Church: Gender, Power, and Organizational Culture* (Oxford: Oxford University Press, 2011). At p. 232 Keenan writes: 'In my analysis of the clerical perpetrators and of child sexual abuse with the Catholic Church (a highly gendered organization), gender, power, and organizational culture are at the heart of the matter.'

men, in the Church's decision-making and particularly in the governing office of the Church is critical in addressing the issue of clericalism.[41]

4 The challenge to the laity

The council has much to say about the responsibilities of the hierarchy and of the clergy more generally in regard to the laity. But it also issues a challenge directly to the laity, many of whom currently fail to recognize and claim their rights and responsibilities as members of the Church. The Council calls on the laity to step up to their baptismal calling. They are called to active participation, not passive presence. They have the duty to accept their share in the responsibility for the mission of the Church and to play their active and constructive parts in it. It is their right and their responsibility to be actively involved in fostering a community of dialogue, mutual esteem and support, and participative decision-making, all in service of the Church's mission.

The Council's teachings prompt serious questions for both ordained and laity as we look to the next chapter of the implementation of the Council's vision: What structures and processes would further facilitate the laity taking up their responsibilities? What education and formation of the laity would advance the laity's understanding and exercise of their rights and duties? What mechanisms would allow the laity's voices to be sought and heard in matters which concern the good of the Church, its life, mission, pastoral practice and doctrinal development? What if the expertise of lay persons with appropriate experience in administration and governance was called on to achieve the much-needed reform of the Roman Curia for which the recent conclave called so clearly? What if the voice of the laity with appropriate competence was sought in regard to practical, pastoral and doctrinal issues now before us as a community? How might the laity be more actively involved and empowered in the management of their own parishes and dioceses? For the bishop, as Pope Francis explained recently, 'has to be among his people in three ways: in front of them, pointing the way; among them, keeping

---

[41] Pope Francis has commented, 'Let us not reduce the involvement of women in the Church, but instead promote their active role in the ecclesial community. By losing women, the Church risks becoming sterile.' See http://en.radiovaticana.va/news/2013/07/28/pope_francis_to_brazilian_bishops:_are_we_still_a_church_capable_of/in2-714616.

them together and preventing them from being scattered; and behind them, ensuring that no one is left behind, but also, and primarily, so that the flock itself can sniff out new paths'.[42] It is time, he suggests, to afford the laity the 'freedom and space to act' (*LG* 37) within their spheres of expertise and to 'sniff out new paths'.

Conclusion

Cardinal Fernando Cento, then president of the Commission for the Lay Apostolate, when introducing the subject of the laity to the Council, reminded the Council Fathers: 'The Laity are not simply *in the Church*, rather, together with us, they *are the Church*, its living, active members.'[43] As Blessed John Henry Newman famously noted, 'The church would look foolish without them.'[44]

The Council's teaching on the laity, their rights and duties, was one of its ground-breaking achievements. In the much expanded vision of the role of the laity which the Council opened up as a corollary of its new ecclesial self-understanding, the Council challenged both the ordained and the laity to a renewed sense of co-responsibility for the shared *koinonia* and mission of the Church and the development of the structures and processes to enable it. Much has been achieved in these last fifty years, but full reception and implementation is yet to be realized. It is understandable that interpretation, reception and implementation is necessarily taking time. The decisive question, as has been recognized,

> is whether we are giving the new ecclesial self-understanding enough time and room to develop its own dynamism and shape, and thus to gain the strength it needs for creatively appropriating tradition and incorporating it into a continuity at a new level. Or, to put it differently, the decisive question is whether we are giving the Spirit of God enough freedom to lead the Church along new paths.[45]

---

[42] Pope Francis, http://en.radiovaticana.va/news/2013/07/29/pope_francis:_address_to_celam_leadership/in2-714915.

[43] Hanjo Sauer, 'The Council Discovers the Laity', in *History of Vatican II*, vol. 4, p. 235.

[44] John Henry Newman, *On Consulting the Faithful in Matters of Doctrine*, pp. 18–19.

[45] Hermann Pottmeyer, 'A New Phase in the Reception of Vatican II: Twenty Years of Interpretation of the Council', p. 34.

In regard to that question, Pope Francis has indeed cautioned against resistance or attempts to tame the Spirit's promptings.[46]

We as a community, as for the Church in every age, are called in our day to respond to the Holy Spirit, who 'dwells in the Church and in the hearts of the faithful' (*LG* 4). We together are called to conversion, a conversion to the vision of Church inspired by the Holy Spirit in the event of the 'great grace'[47] that was the Second Vatican Council. There is so much to be gained, and a great grace to be received, for the Church and for the world.

---

[46] Pope Francis, http://en.radiovaticana.va/news/2013/04/16/pope:_2nd_vatican_council,_work_of_holy_spirit_but_some_want_to_tur/en1-683419.

[47] Pope John Paul II, Apostolic letter, *Novo Millennio Ineunte* (2001), § 57. http://www.vatican.va/holy_father/john_paul_ii/apost_letters/documents/hf_jp-ii_apl_20010106_novo-millennio-ineunte_en.html.

4

From Correlationism to Trinitarian Christocentrism: Receiving the Council in the Church in Australia

Tracey Rowland

The reception of the decrees of any Church Council is usually a traumatic process and Vatican II has been no exception. After the Council of Constantinople in 381, St Gregory of Nazianzus wrote that he was convinced that 'every assembly of bishops is to be avoided', since he had never experienced a 'happy ending to any Council'.[1] St Gregory's friend, St Basil the Great, held a similar judgement. He spoke of the 'shocking disorder and confusion' generated by Church Councils.[2] More recently, Cardinal Mauro Piacenza, who is the Prefect for the Congregation of the Clergy, told an assembly of seminarians in California that theirs would probably be the first generation that will correctly interpret the documents of the Council.[3]

The intellectual interpretations of documents and their subsequent embodiment in cultural practices is such a complex area that German scholars have coined the word *Wirkungsgeschichte* to refer to a whole academic sub-field dedicated to the study of this phenomenon. In other words, this is the study of how documents have been received and interpreted, regardless of the original intentions of the authors. The present work is therefore offering a kind of *Wirkungsgeschichte* of the reception of the documents of the Council in Australia.

---

[1] Gregory Nazianzus, Epistle 130, 'Ad Procopium', cited by Joseph Ratzinger, *Principles of Catholic Theology* (San Francisco: Ignatius, 1987), p. 368.

[2] Ibid., p. 368.

[3] Mauro Cardinal Piacenza, 'Intervento del cardinal Mauro Piacenza, Perfetto della Congregazione per il Clero', Martedi, 4 ottobre 2011, Los Angeles, Incontro con i Seminaristi. Text available in Italian at: www.clerus.org/clerus/dati/2011-09.

In the 1970s, in Catholic parishes and schools, the most obvious effect of the Council was that nuns began to change their names and mode of dress and there was a new Order of the Mass in English. Habits became shorter and less elaborate and it became fashionable for nuns to drop their religious names and revert to their baptismal names. As children, this meant that in one term we could be calling someone Sr Thomas and then after a couple of weeks' holiday we would come back to a new term to be taught by the same person who was now called Sr Christine. The title Mother Superior was often dropped altogether and everyone became merely a sister. Egalitarianism was fashionable. In the convent where I was a boarder, the wooden horseshoe-shaped refectory table was broken up and replaced by a large number of steel framed tables with laminated tops. Whereas the nuns had previously been seated in rank order around the horseshoe with the most junior nuns occupying each extreme end, the new system was that people could sit wherever they liked on any table they liked. The hierarchical seating plan was dropped. Also at this time, there was a tendency for nuns to take on a variety of works outside of the parish school and their convent. This meant that they were not always together for their prayers and people began to pray privately. Not only was Latin dropped as the language of the liturgy but Latin hymns were also discarded and in many parishes and in particular in schools, they were replaced with folk songs. The most notorious of these was Kumbayah, a Gullah chant which hundreds of thousands of Australian Catholic school children were forced to learn, notwithstanding the fact that for most of us, Gullah was not our mother tongue.[4]

These changes were made in accordance with the Conciliar Decree on the Adaptation and Renewal of Religious Life – *Perfectae Caritatis,* especially paragraph three, which read:

The manner of living, praying and working should be suitably adapted everywhere, but especially in mission territories, to the modern physical and psychological circumstances of the members and also, as required by

---

[4]   Gullah is a Pidgin-English-based Creole language spoken by former slaves living on the Sea Islands of South Carolina and Georgia. According to Samuel Freedman of the *New York Times* (20 November 2010), 'No scholar has ever found an indigenous word "kumbayah" with a relevant meaning.' The provenance of the song is a subject of academic controversy. It was highly popular in the 1960s and recorded by many groups and individual artists and is now regarded as 'iconic' of the late 1960s' 'flower-power' era. Why it was so popular in Australian Catholic schools in the 1970s remains an open question.

the nature of each Institute, to the necessities of the apostolate, the demands
of culture, and social and economic circumstances.

The Decree of the Council on the Adaptation and Renewal of Religious Life
liberated Australian religious from many practices that did not transpose well
from the colder European countries like Ireland to the tropical and subtropical
parts of Australia. But it also had the effect of opening up almost every aspect
of the order's life to the possibility of change, since expressions like 'physical,
psychological and socio-economic circumstances' and 'the demands of
culture' are so broad that they can be used to cover a wide variety of practices.
The phrase 'the demands of the local culture' is like an ecclesiastical blank
cheque unless it is underpinned by some kind of theology of culture, but the
expression 'theology of culture' was not known at the time of the Council.

One of the slogans of the 1960s' generation was Bob Dylan's phrase, 'the
times, they are a changin''. There was a general sense that the social order of
the Western world was dying. Religious order after religious order engaged
in long periods of introspection, seeking to determine what elements of
its heritage remained relevant to contemporary culture and what elements
needed to be abandoned. As a consequence, the general ordered rhythm of
the life of those who had taken religious vows started to break down. There
was no longer any certainty. Even the signature works of the individual orders
changed. People who had joined an order that was focused on the education
of children suddenly found themselves in an organization that wanted to
get out of teaching and into social work; others who were members of the
more intellectual orders found that their orders wanted to move out of
universities and into social justice or missionary work; and those involved in
missionary work often began to question whether their approaches had been
too European and if their decades of self-sacrificial service had been counter-
productive. As Cardinal George Pell mentioned in his opening address of
the *Great Grace* conference, the number of Australian nuns has decreased by
63 per cent since the mid-1970s. There were 4,765 nuns in Australia in 2012
compared to 14,622 in 1966.[5]

By the mid-1970s, being a nun no longer seemed like a 'relevant' lifestyle
option. Married women could also have careers and from the early 1960s

---

[5] Verity Edwards, 'Nuns a vanishing breed as few heed calling', *The Australian* (1 April 2013).

universities were popping up in the suburbs to take in thousands of students from upwardly mobile working-class families. For the first time in the history of Australia, a generation of Catholics had the possibility of breaking into the professional class in large numbers. Whereas sectarian rivalry had for generations operated as a barrier to socially aspirational Catholics, with some government departments and many law firms and gentlemen's clubs being closed to Catholics, from the late 1960s onwards this interdenominational rivalry began to break down. This was one of the positive side effects of the Council which had fostered the work of ecumenism. For many Catholics, being able to attend a Protestant friend's wedding was a major post-conciliar reform.

However, these new social opportunities for Catholics operated as a double-edged sword. The American author E. Michael Jones said of the 1960s generation of Catholics in countries with sizeable Protestant populations that they 'lusted after Modernity', meaning that in the United States and the countries of the British Commonwealth, Catholics were tired of being different.[6] They desperately wanted acceptance within the Protestant establishment and they were very eager to shed elements of their Catholic culture that had made them stand apart from their Protestant neighbours. For example, they were very happy when their bishops decided that it was okay for Catholics to eat meat on Friday so long as they did some other form of penance. If they were invited to a BBQ on a Friday they no longer had to make embarrassed apologies. Once the 'no meat on Friday' discipline was dropped, however, most Catholics stopped doing any form of penance on Friday with the consequence that they started to lose a sense of the liturgical dimension of time.

There was a short moment in the 1960s when everyone was euphoric about the Council and especially about ecumenism, and Catholics started to feel as though they were at last socially 'normal'. However, on the 25th of July 1968, Pope Paul VI issued the encyclical *Humanae Vitae* which upheld the Church's teaching against the use of contraceptives. The reaction of many Catholics was one of passive aggression and in some cases, outright opposition. In some countries, theologians placed advertisements in major secular newspapers notifying the laity of their opposition to the encyclical. This was followed in

---

[6] E. Michael Jones, *Living Machines: Bauhaus Architecture as Sexual Ideology* (San Francisco: Ignatius, 1995), p. 42.

1970 by Hans Küng's publication of the book *Infallibility* which called into question the legitimacy of papal authority.

The idea that the Council was all about getting Catholics out of a cultural ghetto by permitting them to embrace the modern world was built on a statement made by St John XXIII to an ambassador who asked him what he hoped to get out of the Council. He replied that he wanted to open the windows and let in some fresh air. Whether Catholics were in fact living in a cultural ghetto in 1960 is a moot point. It seems that the situation varied from country to country and diocese to diocese and even from one social class to another. It is nonetheless generally accepted that in some parts of the world, particularly in Irish Catholic populations, of which we had many in Australia, Catholics did have something of a ghetto mentality, and for these populations the Council was their passport out of the ghetto.

As people scrambled out of the ghetto they became interested in contemporary ideas and practices, and contraception was the revolutionary new social practice of the 1960s generation. The opposition of many of this generation to *Humanae Vitae* was therefore voiced in rhetoric about the purpose of the Council and the proper way to interpret the documents.

In 1970, an international conference was held in Brussels and attended by a large number of those who had been expert theological advisors at the Council. It represented a watershed moment in the history of the reception of the Council because at this conference it became clear that there was a strong division among the experts about the meaning to be given to the Council. In academic parlance, we would say that there were two different metanarratives explaining the purpose of the Council. In academic journals, they are often described in shorthand as the metanarrative of *aggiornamento* and the metanarrative of *ressourcement*.

Aggiornamento is an Italian word meaning renewal, and *ressourcement* is a French word meaning a return to the sources. As a generalization, one can say that the *ressourcement* theologians wanted renewal, and they wanted *aggiornamento*. But not all of those who wanted *aggiornamento* wanted the *ressourcement* recipe for *aggiornamento*. Another way to put this is to say that there was very little agreement about what the content of the renewal should be. One of the leading historians of the Council, John O'Malley, has written that 'at the time of the Council we did not think to ask from it any consistent theoretical foundation for *aggiornamento*, because most of us were not aware of the importance of having one'.[7] O'Malley concluded that 'the Council's fundamental injunction to remain faithful to the authentic past while adjusting to contemporary needs was transformed from a practical norm for reform into an explosive problematic'.[8] One person who was on to the problem quite early was the Protestant theologian Karl Barth. In an interview with Pope Paul VI in 1966, he asked, 'What exactly does *aggiornamento* mean? Accommodation to what?'[9]

The *ressourcement* scholars were highly critical of what they called 'baroque theology', the theological framework that was put together after the Council of Trent. It was forged in the furnace of the civil wars which racked the countries of Europe in the sixteenth and seventeenth centuries. A whole raft of theologians and intellectual historians were in agreement that Francisco Suárez, one of the leading architects of this theological edifice, and other commentators on the works of St Thomas Aquinas in the sixteenth and seventeenth centuries, had not only misinterpreted Thomas Aquinas but that these misinterpretations had opened up the culture of Europe to secularism.[10]

A generation of scholars from the 1940s to the 1960s fought battles within academic institutions both for and against the baroque theological edifice. The politics was deadly and the rhetoric intense. Some scholars, like the French Jesuit Henri de Lubac, found themselves silenced. Others, like the French philosopher and historian Etienne Gilson, referred to baroque era theology as a 'brew of watered-down *philosophia aristotelico-thomistica* concocted to give off a vague deism fit only for the use of right-thinking candidates for high school diplomas' and he described the works of the Dominican Cajetan as in every respect the consummate example of a corruption of the thought of St Thomas.[11] The young Joseph Ratzinger who was to become Pope Benedict XVI was of a similar mind. His Prefect

---

[7] John O'Malley, *Tradition and Transition: Historical Perspectives on Vatican II* (Wilmington: M. Glazier, 1989), p. 45.

[8] John O'Malley, *Tradition and Transition*, p. 67.

[9] Karl Barth, *Ad Limina Apostolorum* (Edinburgh: St. Andrew's Press, 1969), p. 20.

[10] There are many books and articles covering this scholarship, but an accessible and very comprehensive overview may be found in Fergus Kerr's *Twentieth-Century Catholic Theologians* (Oxford: Blackwell, 2006).

[11] Etienne Gilson, *Letters to Henri de Lubac* (San Francisco: Ignatius, 1986), p. 24.

of Studies in his seminary said that pre-conciliar scholasticism 'wasn't his beer'.[12] He almost failed his habilitation thesis because he dared to be critical of the theory of revelation put forward by Suárez. He argued instead for the position of St Bonaventure. Since St Bonaventure is a Doctor of the Church, Ratzinger thought he would be on safe ground, but he only rescued his academic career by ditching those sections of his thesis which were critical of Suárez. In an extraordinary twist of fate, however, at the Second Vatican Council, Ratzinger helped to draft the document *Dei Verbum* which upheld the Christocentrism of St Bonaventure's theory and quietly set aside the Suárezian view of revelation.[13]

At the Council there were therefore three basic factions: First, there were those who wanted to champion the pre-conciliar baroque theological order and therefore who wanted little or no change. Secondly, the *ressourcement* types such as the French Jesuits Henri de Lubac and Jean Daniélou, who wanted change but whose view of change was predominately a revival of neglected elements of patristic thought and a purification of the theological establishment of baroque dualisms. Thirdly, there was a group who wanted change but who were very open to ideas stemming from post-eighteenth-century liberal philosophical sources, and this included Karl Rahner as a champion of what is called Transcendental Thomism, a fusion of Kantian epistemology with elements of classical era Thomism, not baroque era Thomism. Rahner and Ratzinger were very much on the same side in their opposition to Suárezian Thomism.

At the conference in Brussels, the division between the *ressourcement* types and those more open to the liberal tradition hardened, especially against the background of the latter's opposition to *Humanae Vitae*. Joseph Ratzinger was one of those who attended this conference and it represented his final parting of ways with some of the former experts. In 1972, Joseph Ratzinger, Henri de Lubac and Hans Urs von Balthasar founded the journal *Communio* which has subsequently been published in fourteen different languages. It was set up in opposition to *Concilium* which was the flagship journal of those who

---

[12] Alfred Läpple, Interview by Gianni Valente and Pierlucca Azzardo, *30 Days* 1 (2006), p. 60.

[13] For explanations of what is thought to have been wrong with the Suárezian account, see: John Montag, 'Revelation: the False Legacy of Suárez', in John Milbank (ed.), *Radical Orthodoxy* (London: Routledge, 1999), and Peter Candler, *Theology, Rhetoric, Manuduction, or Reading Scripture Together on the Path to God* (Grand Rapids: Eerdmans, 2006).

interpreted the Council in a more liberal way. The English historian Philip Trower has said of the theologians associated with these two journals that since their establishment they have been engaged in a theological star wars.[14] The fallout does eventually land in parishes, but when it does, people are often completely unaware of the origin of the ideas with which they are being hit. Certainly the ideas floated by the cluster of theologians around these two journals represent two very different appropriations of the documents of the Council. Joseph Ratzinger has tended to describe the division as a difference between a 'hermeneutic of rupture' and a 'hermeneutic of reform'. They both agree that there were problems with the pre-conciliar theological establishment and that major reforms were necessary but there is a difference between reforms which represent organic developments or retrievals of hitherto neglected or poorly presented elements of tradition, and reforms which represent a radical break from tradition.

An excellent example of the promotion of a 'hermeneutic of rupture' may be found in an address delivered by Karl Rahner in 1979. After drawing an analogy between the 'decisive break' in the transition from Jewish to Gentile Christianity at the Council of Jerusalem in 49 AD, and what he called the 'decisive break' in the transition from pre-conciliar to post-conciliar Catholicism after the Second Vatican Council, Rahner commented:

> Today, as a matter of fact, perhaps even in contrast to patristic and medieval theology, we do not have a clear, reflective theology of this break, this new beginning of Christianity with Paul as its inaugurator. ... And yet I would venture the thesis that today we are experiencing a break such as occurred only once before, that is, in the transition from Jewish to Gentile Christianity ... such transitions happen for the most part and in the final analysis, unreflectively, they are not first planned out theologically and then put into effect.[15]

A concept which was the hallmark of the *Concilium* style theologians was that of correlationism. This project was promoted by the Flemish Dominican Edward Schillebeeckx, among many others. The idea was to identify what were called toothing stones in the popular culture to which the Catholic faith could

---

[14] Philip Trower, *Turmoil and Truth: The Historical Roots of the Modern Crisis in the Catholic Church* (San Francisco: Ignatius, 2003), p. 32.
[15] Karl Rahner, 'Towards a Fundamental Interpretation of Vatican II', *Theological Studies* 40 (1979), pp. 716–28 (723).

be tied or correlated. Part of the justification for this pastoral strategy was a remark made by John XXIII in his opening address to the Council:

> What is needed is that this certain and immutable doctrine, to which the faithful owe obedience, be studied afresh and reformulated in contemporary terms. For this deposit of faith, or truths which are contained in our time-honored teaching is one thing; the manner in which these truths are set forth (with their meaning preserved intact) is something else.

This statement was popularly interpreted as the idea that the faith needed repackaging. Since the 1960s was a decade of cultural revolution, including the arrival of a youth culture, in many schools and parishes the Council was interpreted as a call to present the Catholic faith to youth in the idioms of pop culture. This is probably not what John XXIII had in mind. He made his speech in October 1962, some fourteen months before the Beatles released 'I Want to Hold Your Hand' and before they left 4,000 screaming teenagers at Heathrow airport on their way to the United States. Pope John was probably thinking that the faith could be expressed in language other than, or at least, in addition to, the Latin scholastic maxims that filled the textbooks of the seminarians. Nonetheless, four years after this opening address, on 22 October 1966, the Jesuit publication *America* carried an article by someone called Gareth Edwards who claimed that the Second Vatican Council's *Constitution on the Liturgy* implied that 'the nearer the language of the Eucharist can be brought to modern vernacular, the greater the resulting benefit' and further 'that our democratic society and informal habits make it necessary for us to think of God as a friend, not as a king'. It would be a great pity, wrote Edwards, 'if, at the moment when it bursts out of the strait jacket of Latin, it allowed itself to be enclosed in that of Anglican English. … If the Church wants to sweep the world like the Beatles, it must use language as contemporary as theirs'.[16]

Three years later, in 1969, Pope Paul VI said something very similar in an address that may be described as his eulogy for what we now call the Extraordinary Form. In this address he described Latin as the language of the angels and he acknowledged that in adopting the Missal of 1969, Catholics were parting with the speech of Christian centuries and behaving like

---

[16] Gareth Edwards, *America* (22 October 1966).

'profane intruders in the literary precincts of sacred utterance'.[17] Nonetheless, he concluded that liturgical participation by the laity is more important than beautiful language, and he noted that modern people are fond of plain language. This, of course, was a highly controversial prudential and largely sociological judgement which to some degree was reversed in the papacy of Benedict XVI with the decree *Summorum Pontificum* and the revision of the English text of the Mass. Today, the pendulum has begun to swing in the direction of beautiful language (both Latin and the vernacular) rather than plain language.

Even in the 1970s, not everyone agreed that correlating the faith and in particular, liturgical language, to whatever happened to be the contemporary cultural norms was a prudent idea. The Sydney-born poet James McAuley was highly critical of this. Although he initially supported the change to the vernacular Mass, he began to feel doubt and regret and he noted that the changes resulted in an immense loss musically. He remarked that it was easy to pull down an old structure but not so easy to put up a new one that has the same integrity of form and style. In an earlier essay on the *End of Modernity*, published on the eve of the Council, he was critical of modernist elements in literature, art and culture generally, and he observed that

> the irony of it is that while the Church seems to ride becalmed in a glucose sea, over which the sinking sun of the Enlightenment spreads its sentimental hues, the tide of secular taste is now flowing in a different direction: contemporary taste is looking with an awakened nostalgia towards the art that societies can produce when they are faithful to their sacred traditions.[18]

McAuley's reference to the sinking sun of the Enlightenment was a poetic way of saying that the Enlightenment, or the philosophy of the eighteenth century, and the culture of modernity it fostered, was on its way out of fashion. In today's marketing terminology we would say that modernity was turning toxic. As even Schilleebeeckx's biggest fans now acknowledge, Catholic intellectuals got excited about modernity just as the rest of the world's intellectual elite gave up on it and turned postmodern. The British journalist Malcolm Muggeridge

---

[17] Paul VI, General Audience Address of 26 November 1969.
[18] James McAuley, *The End of Modernity: Essays on Literature, Art and Culture* (Sydney: Angus and Robertson, 1959), p. 94.

said that it was as if Catholics came out of their trenches with their hands in the air, surrendering to the forces of the Enlightenment only to discover that there was no one waiting to receive their surrender, because the enemy, so to speak, had moved on to another battlefield.

The Canadian philosopher Kenneth Schmitz has also observed that in the 1960s very few Catholic scholars had any understanding of what sociologists now mean by the concept of modernity. Had they been more perceptive, Schmitz suggests, they might have noticed that the foundations of modernity were beginning to crack under an increasingly incisive attack. But most of them had no concept of modernity as a cultural formation, and the only concept they had in their intellectual armoury was the historical category of modern philosophy.[19]

Today, however, most Catholic scholars are familiar with scholarship on the culture of modernity. There is, for example, Alasdair MacIntyre's reading of modernity as the *severance* of the classical-theistic synthesis, the Charles Taylor and Louis Dupré readings of it as a *mutation* of the same synthesis, the Hans Blumenberg reading as the *re-occupation* of defunct Christian concepts with a new non-Christian substance, the Eric Voegelin thesis of modernity as a form of *neo-gnosticism*, and the 'Radical Orthodoxy' reading represented by Catherine Pickstock and John Milbank as the *heretical reconstruction* of the classical-theistic synthesis. Regardless of the differences in nuance between severance, mutation, re-occupation, neo-gnosticism and heretical reconstruction, in each of these accounts of the culture of modernity there is a common agreement that this culture is far from theologically neutral.

Moreover, the so-called 'modern man' who is at home within this culture has been described variously as a 'one-dimensional man' (the verdict of Herbert Marcuse), *an animal producens et consumens* (the verdict of the Czech Jesuit Joseph Zverina), a 'mass man' who has 'no desire for independence or originality' (the assessment of Romano Guardini), a 'deprived and isolated emotivist' (the indictment of Alasdair MacIntyre), a 'micro-cosmic tragedy' who 'doesn't know which team he is playing on' (the judgement of Vaclav Havel), a Hobbesian egoist (the description of Oxford philosopher

---

[19] Kenneth L. Schmitz, 'Postmodernism and the Catholic Tradition', *American Catholic Philosophical Quarterly*, LXXIII, 2 (1996), pp. 223–53 (235).

John Gray) and a new type of barbarian (the conclusion of the philosopher Erazim Kohak), to mention just a few of the descriptions.[20] When one adds the Nietzschean definitions of someone with a 'small soul' and 'herd-like morality' and communitarian criticisms of the 'rootless cosmopolitan' – a being with a highly impoverished historical memory and without loyalties to any traditions, countries, institutions or localities – one rapidly reaches the conclusion that the depiction of anyone as a 'modern man' carries strongly negative connotations.

At the time of the Council, this body of literature was almost entirely unwritten with the exception of Guardini's book *The End of the Modern World*. In his autobiographical work, *A Theologian's Journey*, the Dominican historian Thomas F. O'Meara suggested that much conflict would have been avoided if Romano Guardini's perspectives on modernity had been read by the Council Fathers.[21] It seems that at the time of the Council they were not well known outside of Germany and it was largely French and Belgian scholars who drafted *Gaudium et spes*, not Germans like Rahner and Ratzinger who were enthusiastic students of Guardini.

Thus, somewhat tragically, Catholic theologians who interpreted the Council, especially *Gaudium et spes*, as a call to make the Catholic faith more compatible with the culture of modernity were often unaware of just how far *behind the times* such thinking really was. As Archbishop Augustine Di Noia has noted: 'The Post-Conciliar interpretation of John XXIII's vision of *aggiornamento* as updating theology is, from the perspective of post-modern eyes, a project which has never really caught up, while conceived more grandly as modernization, it is already far behind.'[22]

Today, if one walks into a common room of a great secular university and announces oneself as a species of modernity, people tend to react as if there is a bad smell in the room. The reaction is something like: where have you

---

20 Herbert Marcuse, *One Dimensional Man* (Boston: Beacon Press, 1964); Jozef Zverina as quoted by Rudolf Battek, 'Spiritual values, independent initiatives and politics', in John Keane (ed.), *The Power of the Powerless* (London: Hutchinson, 1985), pp. 97–99; Romano Guardini, *The End of the Modern World* (London: Sheed & Ward, 1957); Alasdair MacIntyre, *After Virtue: A Study in Moral Theory* (London: Duckworth, 1981); Vaclav Havel, 'Politics and Conscience', *Salisbury Review* (January 1985); John Gray, *Liberalism* (London: Open University Press, 1986); and Erazim Kohak, *The Embers and the Stars: A Philosophical Inquiry into the Moral Sense of Nature* (University of Chicago, 1984).

21 Thomas F. O'Meara, *A Theologian's Journey* (Boston: Paulist Press, 2002), p. 218.

22 Augustine Di Noia, 'American Catholic Theology at Century's End: Postconciliar, Postmodern and Post Thomistic', *The Thomist* 54 (1990), pp. 499–518 (518).

been, have you not read Nietzsche, Heidegger, Foucault, Derrida and Vattimo? As a consequence, correlationism is being revamped for postmodern sensibilities. Instead of correlating the faith to the culture of modernity, second-generation Schillebeeckxian theologians are exhorting Catholic educators to re-contextualize the faith with reference to the culture of postmodernity.

In his response to the correlationist interpretation of the Council, Joseph Ratzinger remarked that the Church is not a haberdashery shop that updates its windows with each new passing fashion season. A little less poetically, Fr Robert Barron expressed the same idea in his statement that 'philosophy, ethics and cultural forms do not position Christ, rather Christ positions them and that to understand this principle is to grasp the nettle of the Christian thing'.[23]

The alternative to reading the Council's documents as a call to accommodate, correlate or re-contextualize the faith to the contemporary culture, whatever that might be, is the Trinitarian Christocentric reading. In a preface to his *Theological Highlights of Vatican II*, published in 1966, Joseph Ratzinger argued that the conciliar idea of 'renewal' had a twofold intention – 'its point of reference is contemporary man in his reality and in his world, taken as it is. But the measure of its renewal is Christ, as scripture witnesses Him'. Recalling Pope Paul VI's opening address to the second session of the Council, Ratzinger acknowledged that 'while the accents can be variously placed', what most impressed him was 'how Christ-centric it was'. Moreover, in a commentary on *Gaudium et spes* published in 1969, Ratzinger noted that article two of the Zurich text of *Gaudium et spes* had attempted to justify the whole notion of the Church's dialogue with 'the world' by means of the scriptural reference to reading the signs of the times (Mt. 16.3 and Lk. 12.56). However, this earlier draft, which was heavily influenced by the Latin proverb *vox temporis vox Dei* was, according to Ratzinger, rejected by the Council Fathers as bad exegesis.[24] The point of Christ's statement to the Apostles was that He, Christ, was the sign of their times and Ratzinger at least would argue that their times are also our times. They, like us, live in the period of history between the Incarnation and the return of Christ in glory.

<hr>

[23] Robert Barron, *The Priority of Christ: Toward a Post-Liberal Catholicism* (Grand Rapids: Brazos Press, 2007), p. 341.
[24] Joseph Ratzinger, 'The Dignity of the Human Person', in Herbert Vorgrimler (ed.), *Commentary on the Documents of the Second Vatican Council* (London: Burns and Oates, 1969), p. 115.

The dawning of the Age of Aquarius does not have any theological relevance; it does not alter the deposit of the faith, it does not change what it means to be a Christian.

The idea that 'Christ is the sign of our time' and that Christ is the 'Light of the Nations' was constantly affirmed throughout the papacy of John Paul II. At the 1985 Synod of Bishops which he called to reflect upon the Council's reception, Christ-centredness emerged as one of the key conciliar motifs. Particular reference was made to paragraph 22 of *Gaudium et spes*. According to paragraph 22:

> The Truth is that only in the mystery of the incarnate Word does the mystery of man take on light. For Adam, the first man, was a figure of Him who was to come, namely Christ the Lord. Christ, the final Adam, by the revelation of the mystery of the Father, and His Love, fully reveals man to man himself and makes his supreme calling clear.

The central point of the paragraph is that the human person only understands his or her identity to the extent that he or she is open to a relationship with Christ. Christology is deemed necessary for any adequate understanding of what it means to be human. According to this reading, the point of *Gaudium et spes* was not to accommodate the faith to whatever happened to be fashionable in the contemporary culture, but to affirm certain aspirations of so-called 'modern man', such as the longing for human freedom and self-fulfilment, and to argue that only a Christocentric anthropology has any hope of realizing these legitimate aspirations.

Significantly, the account of the *imago Dei* offered in this paragraph was explicitly Trinitarian, not merely 'theistically coloured'. Cardinal Walter Kasper, among others, has argued that it makes an enormous difference to one's interpretation of *Gaudium et spes* whether one emphasizes the first section of this document which is merely 'theistically coloured' or whether one gives priority to the explicitly Trinitarian anthropology of paragraph 22, which was the most often quoted paragraph from all the conciliar documents in the homilies and speeches of John Paul II.[25]

Ratzinger agreed with Kasper and criticized the merely theistically coloured account which appears in Article 12 of *Gaudium et spes* for 'taking as its

---

[25] Walter Kasper, 'The Theological Anthropology of *Gaudium et spes*', *Communio: International Catholic Review* 23 (1996), pp. 129–40.

starting-point the fiction that it is possible to construct a rational philosophical picture of man intelligible to all and on which all men of goodwill can agree, the actual Christian doctrines being added to this as a sort of crowning conclusion'. The latter then 'tends to appear as a sort of special possession of Christians, which others ought not to make a bone of contention but which at bottom can be ignored'.[26] This approach prompted the question of 'why exactly the reasonable and perfectly free human being described in the first articles was suddenly burdened with the story of Christ'.[27] Ratzinger went on to say that this criticism (the idea that the first section of *Gaudium et spes* seems to imply that the second section is a mere optional extra for Catholics who want to take it) was the basis of the protest against the 'optimism' of the schema, not some 'pessimistic view of the human person' or 'an exaggerated theology of sin'.[28]

The theological anthropology of paragraphs 22 and 24 of *Gaudium et spes* also fed into John Paul II's defence of *Humanae Vitae* as expressed in his *Catechesis on Human Love*. In this *Catechesis*, delivered as a series of Wednesday audience addresses in the early years of his pontificate, anthropology was linked to Trinitarian theology and sexuality was situated within this framework of God's offer of divine filiation. Within this *katological* framework (working downwards from the Trinity to the person), the married couple is raised to the exalted position of being a 'radiant icon of Trinitarian love' and the seal of their marital holiness is viewed as nothing less than a 'supernatural work of art'. To quote Cardinal Marc Ouellet:

> The hour of conjugal and family spirituality is therefore the hour of the transcendence of the self into the image of the Trinity, the hour of becoming a house of God, a home of the Most High, an icon of the Trinity, memory and prophecy of the wonders of salvation history.[29]

This nuptial mystery theology is not only at the centre of the renewal of the Church's theology of marriage but it is also being developed with reference to the sacrament of Holy Orders and the spousal character of religious life in general.

---

[26] Ratzinger, *Commentary on the Documents of the Second Vatican Council*, p. 119.
[27] Ibid., p. 120.
[28] Ibid.
[29] Marc Ouellet, *Divine Likeness: Toward a Trinitarian Anthropology of the Family* (Grand Rapids: Eerdmans, 2006), p. 100.

Trinitarian anthropology was so important to John Paul II's understanding of the theological renewal fostered by the Council that he devoted three of his earliest encyclicals to it. *Redemptor Hominis* focused on the human person's relationship to Christ and was followed by encyclicals on the human person's relationship to God the Father (*Dives in Misericordia*) and God the Holy Spirit (*Dominum et vivificantem*). Taken as a trilogy, these encyclicals sketch the outlines of a whole Trinitarian anthropology that represents one of the most significant theological developments of the post-conciliar era. In *Dives in Misericordia* John Paul II went so far as to assert that linking theo-centrism with anthropocentrism, or we might say, emphasizing the relationship between divinity and humanity, rather than setting the two in opposition to each other, is 'one of the basic principles, perhaps the most important one, of the teaching of the Council'. This Trinitarian Christocentric anthropology is part of the core curriculum of the John Paul II Institute for Marriage and Family which has a campus in Melbourne.

Does this analysis mean that Catholics have to choose between institutions that are Christocentric but introspective or liberal and out-going? A typical *Communio* response would be 'No'. Anyone who is authentically Christocentric will also be concerned about the world. David Schindler, the editor of the English language edition of *Communio*, has expressed the theory in this way:

> The Liturgy and most especially the Eucharist, which effects the continuing sacramental presence of the Son's incarnation, thereby takes its meaning from love, and thus from mission and liberation, as revealed in Jesus. Through Baptism and the Eucharist, Christians receive the reality of Jesus Christ, and are thereby taken into his form: namely, the self-emptying love that is intrinsically missionary, that seeks to pour itself out for all the others.

> [Thus] the meaning of the universal call to holiness [is that] … Christians are to extend the reality of Christ into the world, and thereby to contribute to the sanctification of the world. In and with Christ, they are to become co-redeemers. They do this by transmitting the love of Christ which they have received through the sacramental-liturgical mediation of the Church.

> Christian entry into the world is thereby affected internally by eucharistic love, in the way that a form affects something internally.[30]

---

[30] David L. Schindler, 'Towards a Eucharistic Evangelisation', *Communio: International Catholic Review* 19 (Winter 1992), pp. 549–75 (552–53).

From this perspective, the teachings of the Council will be received most deeply into the Church in Australia when people stop thinking about evangelization as a marketing exercise and the faith as a product to be packaged and correlated and re-contextualized with reference to something else, but rather as a matter of deepening our participation in the life and love of the Trinity and thereby affecting the world internally, from within. This is the approach of the many new ecclesial movements which are one of the most obvious examples of the theological renewal of the Council. There are many such groups operating in dioceses across the country. Those of a charismatic provenance bear witness to the fact that the Christian faith is a faith in a tri-personal God, not a mere deism. Many other groups take the teachings of the Council into family and community life. Collectively, the new ecclesial movements are a major contemporary cause for hope. So too are the rising numbers of vocations to the priesthood and the arrival of new vibrant orders of women religious in Australian dioceses. For example, there are the Dominican Sisters of St Cecilia, the Mercy Sisters from Detroit, Mother Teresa's Missionaries of Charity and the new Immaculata community founded in Sydney and now operating in Tasmania. Throughout Australia, there are also contemplative orders of religious such as the Tyburn nuns and the Carmelites who managed to hold their numbers throughout the years of crisis. Eucharistic adoration is also increasing in popularity. Although initially this was largely a response to requests from World Youth Day veterans for Benediction and Holy Hour services, the practice is now spread through various age groups. In the Archdiocese of Brisbane there is 24-hour adoration, seven days a week, managed by some 400 people, mostly laity.

Negatively, a sign that the Trinitarian Christocentrism of the Council has not yet been fully received in Australia is to be found in the banal mission statements of many Catholic agencies and institutions which talk about fostering a sense of community, being inclusive, providing an education for the future, producing the leaders of tomorrow who will care for the welfare of others and so on. If one reads the mission statements of many ostensibly Catholic institutions, they make claims that could equally be held by any benevolent secular institution. Atheists are always keen to point out that the Church does not have a monopoly on philanthropy and at times one senses that Catholic institutions are a little embarrassed about their Christocentric difference and that they make extraordinary efforts to blend in with all the other non-Christian philanthropic associations. It was perhaps in a reaction against this kind of mentality that Pope Francis in one of his earliest homilies warned that the Church was in danger of being regarded as a mere charity. While it is true that the Church performs many excellent works of charity and that these are a part of her mission, it is always important to show how a Christian approach to charity, or education or health care is different from secular charities, educational institutions and hospitals.

When our mission statements start to say that our institutions exist to foster the humanism of the Incarnation or to produce graduates who participate in the life and love of the Holy Trinity through the agency of the Church as the universal sacrament of salvation, or in the case of hospitals, to serve the sick as if they were Christ himself, when, in one institution after another, we acknowledge that our reason for being is to foster a Trinitarian Christocentric civilization of love, and direct our actions to that end, then the great grace of the Council might have a chance to break through the layers of bureaucratic secularism which in many places continue to impede its reception.

5

Vatican II: Spirit and Letter

Anthony Kelly CSsR

To appreciate the 'great grace' of the Second Vatican Council, two terms are unavoidable: 'spirit' and 'letter'. Are they opposites? Can one be used against the other? Are they complementary? Do they express different perspectives on Vatican II as a still unfolding event in the life of the Church?

The 'letter' of the sixteen conciliar documents is there in black and white.[1] Fifty years later, these documents continue to make us ask how they might be best presented, more precisely translated and best received. After all, the world in which they were written is a world that has rapidly and vastly changed – there was no internet then, and the Soviet Union was the bastion of atheistic communism. And since that time, we have had a Polish, then a German and now an Argentinian pope. The first two participated in the Council, but Pope Francis did not: he was not one of the 'Council Fathers'. That will give a new complexion to our theme. In the meantime, it is instructive to ponder on how the times have changed, and how that affects our reading of Vatican II.

In other words, the question of the 'spirit' of the Council arises: obviously it has to be beholden to the 'letter'; and yet it would be a distortion to be so fixated on the 'letter' as to be without a sense of the larger event that was occurring, and of the way the Holy Spirit was, and is, acting. When the 'letter' is read in the wrong spirit, a war of words can easily result, with no one the wiser.

My topic, 'Vatican II: Spirit and Letter', has been quite contentious. These terms, 'letter' and 'spirit', however unavoidable, can be mischievously opposed. By upholding the letter, it is argued, the less you allow for the spirit. Or, in

---

[1] Standard commentaries are H. Vorgrimler (ed.), *Commentary on the Documents of Vatican II* (5 vols; New York: Herder and Herder, 1967–69); Peter Hünnermann and B. Jochen Hilberath, *Herder theologischer Kommentar zum zweiten Vatikanischen Konzil* (5 vols; Freiburg i/Br: Herder, 2004–06). For further developments, see James L. Heft with John O'Malley (eds.), *After Vatican II: Trajectories and Hermeneutics* (Grand Rapids Michegan: Eerdmans, 2012).

contradiction, the more you go with the spirit, the less you need to be beholden to the letter. While both extremes are clearly silly, 'letter' and 'spirit', in fact, are not simply complementary. There is always room for discussion as to what a given text might mean, even in regard to our most sacred biblical texts. But it does help, in interpreting scripture or the documents of the Council, to suppose, like the author of John's Gospel, that, if we try to pin down the Word incarnate, 'the world itself could not contain the books that would be written' (Jn 21.25). Similarly, the 'right spirit', in its deepest meaning, leads to adoration of the Holy Spirit, inspiring and guiding us into an ever deeper union with Christ in the love of God and love of neighbour.

A discernment of spirits is necessary.[2] There can never be a complete interpretation in every instance. The many possible connotations and correlations of 'letter' and 'spirit' suggest that there are many possible perspectives on the event of Vatican II as we look back on these fifty years. Vatican II, in letter and in spirit, is still a living issue. It is an inexhaustible event still unfolding in the life of the Church and refreshing Christian faith in every age. The *aggiornamento* it represents in the language of St John XXIII is not best translated as 'adjournment'!

What happened fifty years ago can stir deeper memories, refresh hopes, inspire energy; and allow room to express regrets, too. For example, as a member of a religious order, and recalling the conflicts that divided our communities, I find myself asking whether the invocation of Vatican II for or against this issue or that needed to have occasioned so much conflict and so much pain. Did a partisan ideology creep into our conferences and common rooms to make us forget a gracious sense of proportion, and perhaps even lose something of that wonderful grace, a sense of humour? A prickly Catholic form of political correctness made the play of conversation very difficult.

But that came later. Those of us who were in Rome in those days can easily recall the excitement of the time. Though our Church history lecturer had assured his students that there would never be another ecumenical council, here we were, and the Second Vatican Council was happening, and members of our different communities were participating in it. In my case, there was

---

[2] Massimo Faggioli, 'Between Documents and Spirit: The Case of "the New Catholic Movements"', in Heft and O'Malley (eds.), *After Vatican II*, 1–22, especially pp. 20–22.

the direct and excited participation of the great Bernard Häring, CSsR and the less direct but more informative communications of Francis X. Murphy, CSsR – known to the world under the pseudonym Xavier Rynne. Excitement was in the air; *Time* magazine ran an informed report every week. Every evening in this college or that, distinguished theologians involved in the Council addressed groups of students and clergy – all bright bubbles in the general ebullience of the time.

When the conciliar sessions ended, Pope Paul VI's farewell to the Council Fathers on 8 December 1965 was memorable. He held together both the letter and spirit of Vatican II as he looked ahead, and his words can still stir us these many years later. He prayed:

> [that] a new spark of divine charity may rise in our hearts … that it may really produce in the Church and in the world that renewal of thoughts, activities, conduct, moral force and hope and joy which was the very scope of the council.

Pope Paul goes on:

> The hour for departure and separation has sounded. In a few moments you are about to leave the council assembly to go out to meet mankind and to bring the good news of the Gospel of Christ and of the renewal of His Church at which we have been working together for four years.

Clearly, the Council was a point of departure, not only a point of arrival for those who came and participated. Let us take a moment to ponder upon the world that was emerging.

Fifty years or so have gone by, and many changes have occurred. It is a strange aspect of time-bound human experience, and especially when it comes to great events, that one often does not know what is really going on. That has to be left to history, and that is always open to revision, as we are finding out with so many interpretations of 'what happened at Vatican II' – the title of an influential book by the well-known Church historian, John O'Malley, S. J., with a special interest in ecumenical councils.[3]

The 'Church in the Modern World' of the late 60s of the century past is now the Church in the so-called 'postmodern' world as we move further into

---

[3] John O'Malley, S. J., *What Happened at Vatican II?* (London: Harvard University Press, 2008).

the present millennium. The largely affirmative approach to the world of, say, *Gaudium et spes*, has yielded a more troubling relationship. It could be that the Council's positive affirmation of the world led us to expect that loving the worldwide neighbourhood in the name of God would make the world love the Church in return. Disappointment resulted.

Further, there are issues too numerous to list in this postmodern world. Perhaps they are best summed up in the new 'isms' – terrorism, consumerism, globalism, feminism, the new atheism (and its attendant anti-humanism), new nationalisms; and more positively, the massive concerns of planetary ecology, of social inclusiveness, especially in relation to women, and the urgent need for global financial reorganization, and for a new configuration of international structures of governance and collaboration.

The world in which the Council documents were written is a world that has rapidly and vastly changed, and in ways the Council Fathers could not have predicted: there was no internet then, none of the computers that we take for granted, or even copying machines as we now know them. The atheism that the Council envisaged was that of the Soviet-sponsored kind. Though the Soviet empire has crumbled, atheism has taken on a virulent Western form in post-Christian cultures. Of course, the crisis of *Humanae Vitae* was looming, but the current demographic crisis of Western countries was hardly imaginable, as indeed was the recognition of same-sex marriage in many countries of the Western world.

A changed world, indeed: we have had a Polish pope, and then a German one and now an Argentinian. But Francis did not participate in the Council as JPII and BXVI had. That will no doubt make a difference in emphasis and interpretation. As Chancellor Bismark once remarked, if you like sausages and respect the law it is best not to be around when either of them is being made. That goes for the production of conciliar documents as well.

What was happening? Here is an interesting point that came home to me through my experience on the International Theological Commission for the last nine years. The teaching Church had to respond to an intriguing problem. In the 1950s, the doctrine of Limbo was in possession: it taught the necessity of baptism for salvation – with Limbo being the fate of all who died without baptism through no fault of their own. The Council decided not to give any ruling on this matter which was beginning to be questioned on many fronts.

After the Council ended, two decades went by, but then, in the mid-1980s a liturgy appeared for children who died without baptism. Then, ten years after that, in 1996 the authoritative *Catechism of the Catholic Church* observed:

> As regards children who have died without baptism, the Church can only entrust them to the mercy of God, as she does in her funeral rites for them. (n. 261, 321)

Now, something was going on in the mind and heart of the Church to explain such a change. The ITC, to its initial embarrassment, was asked to explain what it was. The eventual conclusion was that not only has there been a change of attitude and a development of doctrine, but also an expansion of hope – the hope of the Church opening itself to the immeasurable dimensions of God's will to save all, to place no limits on God's saving mercy.[4] As Thérèse of Lisieux, now a Doctor of the Church, used to say, 'my hopes touch upon the infinite'.[5] Vatican II puts this a different way: for all there is 'the possibility of being made participants, *in a way known only to God*, in the paschal mystery' (*GS* 22; cf. *LG* 8–9).

And so a question: should the event of Vatican II, along with questions of letter and spirit, be viewed as fundamentally arising from and leading into a development of hope; of hope against hope, of hope in the infinities of God's love and mercy?[6] Does that development indicate the deep current of the Church's life in the spirit from which the event of Vatican II arose? I think so.

Event

In the meantime, Vatican II was an event of a special kind. Its impact is still unfolding, brimming over the letter of its documents and more creative

---

[4] See 'The Hope of Salvation for Infants who die without being Baptised', *International Theological Commission*, p. 207.

[5] Her words: 'mes espérances qui touchent à l'infini', in Lettre A, Soeur Marie du Sacré Coeur, Manuscrit (B 2v, 28) in *Sainte Thérèse de l'Enfant-Jésus et de la Sainte-Face: Oeuvres Complètes* (Paris : Cerf-Desclée de Brouwer, 1992), p. 224.

[6] Note, too, the importance of other moments and gestures that throw light on the Council: the invitation to lay and Protestant observers, Paul VI's gift of the papal crown to the poor, his visits to Israel, India and the United Nations, and the gift of a Vatican reliquary of St Andrew to the Greek Orthodox Church (cf. Ormond Rush, 'Toward a Comprehensive Interpretation of the Council and Its Documents', *Theological Studies* 73.3 (September 2012), pp. 547–69 (552)).

than the spirit of any one era. Of course, there are different kinds of events. Some are simply organized and coordinated, to be factually recorded, an occurrence with no particular widespread impact. But there are also events of a more significant and life-changing kind. According to such modern French philosophers as Jean-Luc Marion and Claude Romano, such events are a fascinating and inexhaustible phenomenon. For Christians, the singular instance is the resurrection of the crucified one: when will its influence come to an end? It goes beyond all previous calculations. It intimately involves those caught up in it, so as to lead them to world-changing decisions. The meaning of life is changed. Jesus' rising from the tomb breaks out of anything we might predict or control. There are other instances: a world war, or on a lesser scale, those very human events that are transformative in their impact: a Damascus-like conversion, a devastating grief or failure, falling in love, the sudden discovery of a vocation – even your own birth!

Philosophers point out that such events give rise to a certain 'anarchy'. The fixed points of one's life are dramatically shifted. As a result, the full significance of the event in question can only emerge with time, as the future unfolds.[7] The bigger the event, the more the self is caught up in an incalculable movement within a world newly understood beyond any previous horizon.

Might we suggest, then, that Vatican II was an event in this sense?[8] Something new has broken out, or in. It had consequences. Perhaps sadder and wiser, we found that reform is a perilous business. Imagine how acute observers in past decades from, say, the Soviet Union or apartheid South Africa, or China, or from any worldwide institution for that matter, or even a political party, would have had good reason to observe – and not without trepidation – how change was initiated in the Catholic Church – and what continues to be the outcome – even in a gathering such as this fifty years later. What for the Church can lead to a purified faith and an ever-growing hope in the infinities of God's wisdom and love, might be for other institutions a descent into terminal chaos. Sociologists have found all this quite fascinating.

Although the mixture is still in solution, a great event is being worked out. The words of a young theologian then assisting in the preparation of the

---

[7] For a profound philosophy of events, see especially Claude Romano, *L'événement et le monde*. Essais Philosophiques (Paris: Presses Universitaires de France, 1998), pp. 60–69.

[8] Joseph Ratzinger, *Theological Highlights of Vatican II* (New York: Paulist, 2009).

Council documents give some indication of how this particular event was experienced:

> The spiritual awakening, which the bishops accomplished in full view of the Church, or, rather accomplished *as* the Church, was the great and irrevocable event of the council. It was more important in many respects than the texts it passed.[9]

And yet there are the sixteen documents of the Council. Commentators have long remarked how they introduced a new style in Church teaching. We now pass on to consider this more fully.

A new style

As we recall the event of Vatican II these fifty years later, we are beginning to understand in some way how 'the teaching Church' was experiencing a crash course in also being 'the learning Church', and how the conciliar Fathers learnt how to be the Council they wanted to be. The teaching character of the Church is deeply embedded in Catholic consciousness. Not so developed is our awareness of the Church as learning: reflecting on its own faith, reading the signs of the times, and learning from the best contemporary science and scholarship while encountering other cultures, other traditions and even other religions. To that degree, Vatican II has placed us as a learning Church within a learning world.

Indeed, as the world of human experience was newly valued, the frontiers of Church and world were less clearly defined. Under the luminous sky of the infinite mystery of God, new perspectives were possible in discovering – and suffering – what it means to be the 'Catholic' Church. Such a challenge unsettlingly reaches even to these shores – where Christmas is in summer, Easter is in autumn, the south wind blows cold and where the original inhabitants of this land claim a past history of at least forty millennia; and when all the present inhabitants of this country are being awkwardly confronted with the teeming populations of Asia and its rich variety of ancient cultures. It is no longer a case of Australia being hermetically sealed in its cultural and

---

[9] Ratzinger, *Theological Highlights of Vatican II*, p. 194.

geographical isolation. Australians are provoked into absorbing new realities of a multi-ethnic, multi-religious kind.[10]

What, then, are the qualities of this new style that affect our appreciation of both letter and spirit of the conciliar documents? Within the interplay of letter and spirit, the Council saw itself as 'pastoral'. It sought to speak a language of living faith in the Christian community. It expressed a sense of *solidarity* with the world, at a deep level of experience and communication, both personal and interpersonal. It was a language of freedom and responsibility, of participation and involvement. You might say that such a change turned the customary language of the Church inside out in order to speak more inspiringly of the shared life of grace pulsing within the whole People of God. Another way of expressing this change is to note the conciliar effort to make the great doctrines of faith *heartfelt* in experience and expression. The language style or rhetoric of Vatican II was identity-forming, community-forming and mission-forming. It was the confident language of the People of God, and of the Body of Christ. It was less concerned with defending itself against others, and more intent on reaching out to them and communicating in the tones of all-inclusive grace. As Sir Humphrey in *Yes Minister* would say, such an aim was 'very courageous'. Ormon Rush draws our attention to a German commentator, Christoph Theobald:

> From revelation to the signs of the times, from marriage to international peace, from education and the communications media to ecumenical and interfaith dialogue, from the nature and mission of the Church to the redefinitions of its various functions, ministries and states of life, the bishops managed to depict a renewed vision of Christianity on a planet embarking on globalisation, even to put forward a program of reform that exceeds anything we might have dared imagine earlier. None of the twenty preceding councils showed so much daring and ambition.[11]

Change, however, is not only a matter of style, however welcome that might be. It may be the result of learning from past mistakes and grasping present

---

[10] For a variety of Australian and regional perspectives, see Neil Ormerod, Ormond Rush, David Pascoe, Clare Johnson and Joel Hodge (eds.), *Vatican II: Reception and Implementation in the Australian Church* (Mulgrave, Vic: Garrett Publishing, 2013).

[11] Christoph Theobald, 'The Theological Options of Vatican II', in Alberto Melloni and Christoph Theobald (eds.), *Vatican II: A Forgotten Future* (London: SCM 2005), p. 87 – quoted by Ormond Rush in his 'Toward a Comprehensive Interpretation of the Council and its Documents', *Theological Studies* 73.3 (September 2012), pp. 547–69 (565 n. 59).

opportunities. It may result from new areas of knowledge – from psychology, say, or ecology or astrophysics. It may result from returning to the classic sources of scripture and tradition with new questions, or it may come about through something else, a radical change of mind and heart, as we shall soon suggest.

In that regard, we should note that both recent popes continued, each in his own way, with the new style of thought and expression introduced by the Council, in contrast with the scholastic, doctrinal and Neo-Thomistic language and categories of previous Church documents. For instance, John Paul II introduced phenomenological and existential language into papal documents that might have caused conservative eyebrows to rise, and Benedict XVI's emphasis on St Augustine and St Bonaventure was not the usual style.

To describe the change that the Council wished to bring about, a rather extensive vocabulary was employed, such as *aggiornamento, ressourcement,* reform, renewal, review, etc. Here we learn from the writings of Josef Ratzinger (Benedict XVI), Walter Kasper, Karl Lehman, Giuseppe Alberigo, Hermann Pottmeyer, Joseph Komonchak, John O'Malley and many others, including eminent Australian commentators such as those represented by the editors Neil Ormerod, Ormond Rush, David Pascoe, Clare Johnson and Joel Hodge in the book *Vatican II: Reception and Implementation in the Australian Church,* along with its twenty one contributors. In attending to the kinds of change in evidence, these authors focused on questions of continuity and discontinuity in the life of the Church. Pope Benedict, in his address to the Roman Curia on 22 December 2005, argued that all such discussion is related to an understanding of realistic *reform.*[12] Ormond Rush has written extensively on what that means, and enunciated some six principles in his long article in *Theological Studies.*[13] In brief, a proper interpretation of the letter and spirit of Vatican II must allow for the Council's:

1. historical setting and context;
2. pastoral orientation;
3. intention to proclaim the good news of God's love to all;

---

[12] See Gerald O'Collins, S. J., 'Does Vatican II Represent Continuity or Discontinuity?', *Theological Studies* 74.1 (2012), pp 768–94.

[13] Rush, 'Toward a Comprehensive Interpretation of the Council and its Documents', pp. 547–69.

4. creative retrieval of the past;

5. vision of the Church as the sacrament of salvation;

6. ongoing reception of the its message in the present.

These six principles need to be kept in mind in every attempt to express what the Council meant on any question that might arise. To omit any one of these principles is to be left with a distorted image. There is also another important consideration, to which we now turn.

Conversion

Not many speak about conversion in relation to the Council. Perhaps it was thought to be too individual or too dramatic, and even too theological, since it is not something brought about by human contrivance. All agree that conversion depends on the gift of God. Nonetheless, I would suggest that there is evidence of a great conversion afoot. It is surely a feature of the 'great grace' and makes its presence felt as a continuing corporate invitation to make our own, in mind and heart, the letter and spirit of the Council.

In this regard, the noted Jesuit philosopher-theologian Bernard Lonergan understood the notion of conversion as a multi-dimensional event. Essential to it is the change to a new horizon. He writes of this in the following words:

> The new horizon, though notably deeper, broader and richer, none the less it is also possible that the movement into a new horizon involves an about-face; it comes out of the old by repudiating characteristic features; it begins a new sequence that can keep revealing ever greater depth and breadth and wealth. Such an about-face and new beginning is what is meant by a conversion.[14]

Beyond its immediately religious significance, conversion connotes radical change on the moral, intellectual and even psychological level. We offer a brief word on each of these four levels of conversion for each one throws some light on what went on and is still going forward in the unfolding event of Vatican II.

---

[14] Bernard Lonergan, *Method in Theology* (London: DLT, 1972), pp. 237–39.

First, the religious focus of conversion. This spiritual dimension has to have something to do with an awakening to the infinite mystery of God. Anne Hunt has written on the 'Trinitarian Depths of Vatican II'.[15] She quotes with approval the words of the noted historian of the Council, Giuseppe Alberigo: 'It does not seem an exaggeration to claim that the action of the Spirit and the dynamism of the Trinity were a constant running through the Council itself and the body of its decrees.'[16] That is a good point: many past Councils offered austerely valuable declarations on the Trinity in the interests of doctrinal clarity. But as Professor Hunt has shown and Alberigo observed, a Trinitarian sense of life, community and mission permeated the teaching of this 21st ecumenical Council, and even its understanding of dialogue. Hunt also cites Gregory Baum and the then Josef Ratzinger,[17] both remarking on the extraordinary effervescence that many who caught the spirit of the Council felt, and indeed felt the Holy Spirit to be at work at a privileged time of renewal, reform and conversion. To this degree, faith is not simply giving assent to revealed doctrines, but a response to Christ, through the power of the Spirit, to the saving design and loving presence of the Father. To that degree, this Council was not teaching *about* the Trinity, but was teaching about the Church and the world *from within* its lived sense of the Trinity as the milieu of its deepest, widest, richest life.[18]

But religious conversion has moral consequences. It disarms the heart. This is evident in Vatican II, even though, strictly speaking, the Council said little about moral theology.[19] I have, however, already mentioned how Vatican II evidenced a growth in hope; there was also a wonderful expansion in charity – there comes a time when defending oneself against all-encompassing enemies is stifling. Clearly, the Council decided it was time to view the world not as a battlefield, nor to retire behind the parapets, nor to wander in some kind of spiritual no-man's land. It decided to disarm, as it were, to move out in peace and reconciliation, in healing and forgiveness (and as a consequence, asking forgiveness). It moved towards our separated fellow Christians, to the Jewish

---

¹⁵ Anne Hunt, 'The Trinitarian Depths of Vatican II', *Theological Studies* 74.1 (March 2013), pp. 3–19.
¹⁶ Hunt, 'The Trinitarian Depths of Vatican II', p. 3.
¹⁷ Ibid., pp. 36–37.
¹⁸ See also, Rush, 'Toward a Comprehensive Interpretation', pp. 568–69.
¹⁹ Darlene Fozard Weaver, 'Vatican II and Moral Theology', pp. 23–42; and M. Cathleen Kaveny, 'The Spirit of Vatican II and Moral Theology', pp. 43–67, in Heft and O'Malley (eds.), *After Vatican II*.

people, to all religious believers, and to the secular thinkers of our age, even to the agnostic and the atheist.

Closely connected to a deeper turning towards God and a more generous love for our neighbour is an intellectual conversion of some kind. True, Vatican II is not offering a seminar in philosophy, but that does not mean it was an exercise in mindless piety. Faith brings its own evidence, its own intellectual resources, and its own sense of reality, as the great theologians and Doctors of the Church continually remind us. There are new things to understand, and old things to be newly understood. In the conciliar documents, there is a kind of refreshing open-mindedness in evidence, as though the Church realized that the infinite wisdom of God deserved the keenest intelligence and the deepest commitment to learn on our part. Hence, it spoke of 'reading the signs of the times', in appreciation of God's providence at work in this time, and then, in the conduct of her mission, of the Church being able to learn from the world[20] – which would include learning from other cultures and other religious traditions, to say nothing of a continuing retrieval of the wisdom of the past hidden in her history. You might think that talking of an intellectual conversion is too strong a term to describe what was going on, but at least it suggests the genuine effort to see things differently, to appreciate the Other with a heart disarmed and with an open and humble mind, implying both a greater attention to the voices of the past (*ressourcement*) and a new sensitivity to those of the present day (*aggiornamento*).

But then, there is another dimension of conversion – the psychological, for it suggests a fresh sense of vocation, of calling and mission. In the universal call to corporate and personal holiness in *Lumen Gentium* (*LG* 40), we find the most direct appeal to the heart and its experience of the grace of God and faith in Christ.[21] It is a call to a profoundly human kind of holiness as is evident in the well-known words at the beginning of *Gaudium et spes* (*GS* 1):

> The joy and the hope, the grief and anguish of the people of our time, especially of those who are poor or afflicted in any way, are the joy and the hope, the grief and the anguish of the followers of Christ as well. Nothing that is genuinely human fails to find and echo in their hearts.

---

[20] *Gaudium et spes*, p. 44.

[21] 'All Christians in any state or walk of life are called to the fullness of Christian life and the perfection of love, and by this holiness a more human manner of life is fostered also in earthly society' (*Lumen Gentium* 40, n.r. 2).

The call to holiness shows a sense of solidarity with all human beings and that is based in the Incarnation itself. Christ 'fully reveals man to himself' (cf. *GS* 22, 38), and spurs us on to the energies of hope and love for the world as a whole (*GS* 39). A striking summary statement brings together what we have been suggesting about the manifold conversion at work in the Council and still at work today:

> The Word of God, through whom all things were made, was made flesh, so that as perfect man he could save all men, and sum up all things in himself. The Lord is the goal of human history, the focal point of the desires of history and civilisation, the centre of mankind, the joy of all hearts, the fulfilment of all aspirations. … Animated and drawn together in his Spirit, we press onward on our journey toward the consummation of history which fully corresponds to the plan of his love, 'to unite all things in him, things in heaven and things on earth'. (Eph. 1.10) [*GS* 45 n. 2]

Conclusion

Such words are a continuing reminder that the great grace of Vatican II gives a new meaning to both letter and spirit. A useful way of combining the values of both is to ask: how was our *spirituality* affected by this Council? Our way of praying? Our sense of God? Our understanding of Christ and the Holy Spirit? The meaning of the Christian vocation in the Church and in the world? More radically still, what continuing conversion of mind, heart and imagination is the Spirit inspiring? No single answer will be adequate, but every effort to answer such questions can make for a deeper appreciation of the 'great grace' of Vatican II.

Beyond the letter of the documents we must keep in mind the Word incarnate which no words can contain, and go deeper than any spirit of interpretation to the Holy Spirit who reveals ever fuller dimensions of the mystery of Christ. In the words of the Council's final message to thinkers and scientists, 'May [we] seek the light of tomorrow with the light of today until [we] reach the fullness of light.'

Let me conclude with the Council's message to youth and to the young of heart. In December 1965, we listeners were young but have now grown old. Still, these words encourage us to renew the joy of our youth in other ways:

The Church possesses what constitutes the strength and the charm of youth, that is to say the ability to rejoice with what is beginning, to give ourselves unreservedly, to renew one's self and to set out again for new adventures. … Look upon the Church and you will find in her the face of Christ. … It is in the name of Christ that we salute you, exhort and bless you.

May we each and all receive that blessing and be renewed in its strength.

6

Mission to the Media: Lessons from Catholic Voices

Austen Ivereigh and Jack Valero

Catholic Voices, a British project created in 2010 and now present in fifteen countries, was born out of a disastrous debate held in London the year before on the motion: 'The Catholic Church is a force for good in the world.'

Jack went with a non-Catholic friend curious to hear the arguments on either side. As they walked into the packed hall they were asked to declare if they were in favour or against the motion. Before the speeches, the results were read out: 1,102 against and 678 in favour, with 346 undecided. After the speeches, there was a fresh round of voting. Now just 268 were in favour, with 1,876 against. Jack's friend told him: 'It seems that the more that Catholics speak, the more that people hate the Church.'

Sure, the two speakers against – the author and polemicist Christopher Hitchens and the actor Stephen Fry – were finer debaters. But it was not just about rhetoric and skill. There was an existing predisposition against the Church, clear in the pre-speech votes, which the 'anti' speakers were able to exploit and which the 'pro' speakers unwillingly reinforced. To put this in a formula we later developed, there were unconscious assumptions ('frames') present even before anyone had opened their mouths, and the Catholics were unable to 'reframe' in order to be heard. As they told of the good work being done by the Church in Africa, the audience could only think of the millions dying of AIDS because of the dogmatic Catholic position on contraception.

As we were discussing the debate, Pope Benedict XVI's UK visit was announced. We could see what was coming down the tracks: massive public attention on the kind of hot topic issues which in that debate proved so disastrous for the Church, and Catholics responding either by fleeing the heat or standing and fighting with well-worn weapons of defensiveness and anger. It would not be pretty.

The idea

What to do? We had worked together on a communications project in 2006 in response to the film of Dan Brown's blockbuster *The Da Vinci Code*. Our 'Da Vinci Code Response Group', which was inspired by Opus Dei's strategic response to the movie, had taught us some important lessons.[1] The first was that where there is controversy, there is media interest, and therefore an opportunity to communicate. The second was that we had to understand the indignation of anti-Catholic criticism, because it was rooted, usually, in misapprehension. Third, we needed to be flexible, transparent and available, for news is a frenetic business, and if you can go with its flow you are much more likely to be invited into studios.

For *The Da Vinci Code* we had created a small team of media-friendly, studio-ready speakers who had been a hit with the TV and radio news programmes in the run-up to the film's release. Producers liked our lack of defensiveness, and our willingness to discuss absolutely anything that was put to us, however bizarre or 'offensive'. The *Da Vinci Code* was, for millions, the closest they had come to the Jesus story, and we had an opportunity to share with millions the true story – or at least invite people to look further than Dan Brown's bogus myths.

We decided to use the same approach for the papal visit. But rather than a bureau of 'experts' – professional Catholics with expertise – we wanted people whom the media normally never hears from: 'ordinary' – that is, not expert – young, committed, lay Catholics who could speak on behalf of other mainstream Catholics, rather than as spokespeople for the institutional Church. We would do this not because we were opposed to, or out of step with,

---

[1] See Juan Manuel Mora, the architect of the strategy: *The Catholic Church, Opus Dei and the Da Vinci Code: A Global Communications Case Study* (Rome: Pontifical University of the Holy Cross, 2011). On the 'Da Vinci Code Response Group' as a precursor of Catholic Voices see Jack Valero and Austen Ivereigh, *Who Know Where They Stand: Catholic Voices and the Papal Visit to the UK* (Rome: Pontifical University of the Holy Cross, 2011).

or calling for change in the institution, but for the opposite reason: because we loved the Church, thought with it and were faithful to it. That would be the starting point of the speakers we recruited. And we would teach them some of the art and craft of communicating the Church to a postmodern culture.

Catholic Voices, in other words, started from an idea that to many at the time (and since) seemed odd, if not paradoxical. It would be operationally independent of the bishops while being loyal to them and to Church teaching. The speakers would be authoritative, rather than official, communicators, not seeking to replace the Church's official spokespeople but rather reaching the parts of the audience that they did not – the many radio and TV programmes (and by extension, debating organizations, etc.) which simply needed a 'Catholic case' to be eloquently put. It would need a high degree of trust on the part of the hierarchy, and on our side, a solid formation and the guidance of a chaplain. It was, in fact, the kind of lay initiative that Vatican II envisaged but which has been all too rare.

The lay vocation to evangelize

When the First Vatican Council closed in 1870, the most contentious issue was papal infallibility, and that is what history associates with it. Yet papal infallibility has only been invoked once since then, and has otherwise had little effect in the life of the Church. A much more important change in the decades between Vatican I and Vatican II was the gradual wresting of control of the Church from the secular authorities, reserving for itself, for example, the appointment of bishops. In the early twentieth century, the Church became the master of its own destiny.

The controversial topics at the close of Vatican II were the liturgy, together with the unresolved issue of collegiality. But it is worth asking if, 100 years after Vatican II, historians will agree that those were the areas with the greatest impact on the Church. Perhaps the most significant shift will not be in liturgy or the balance between Rome and Bishops' Conferences, but will instead lie in the energizing of lay Catholics to evangelize the world, as they assimilate the true meaning of the universal call to holiness. It is something that has really only just begun.

Before the Council, the Church was conceived in terms of the pope as successor of St Peter and the bishops as successors of the Apostles. Then came priests and deacons, who were in Holy Orders; followed by the religious men and women, who had taken special vows and lived consecrated lives; and last came the laity, defined as 'none of the above'. But *Lumen Gentium* turned this around. Already in Chapter II the document spoke of the People of God, Christ's faithful, before speaking of the hierarchy in the following chapter. And most significantly, it explained that the laity had a special function which belonged only to them.

> The laity, by *their very vocation*, seek the kingdom of God by engaging in temporal affairs and by ordering them according to the plan of God. They live in the world, that is, in each and in all of the secular professions and occupations. They live in the ordinary circumstances of family and social life, from which the very web of their existence is woven. They are called there by God that by exercising their *proper function* and led by the spirit of the Gospel they may work for *the sanctification of the world from within as a leaven.* (*LG* 31, emphasis added)

Their role, in union with the Church as a whole, was to evangelize the world. A year later, in the decree on the apostolate of the laity, it was made clear that this apostolic mandate came to lay people directly from God through baptism, not mandated through the hierarchy:

> The laity derive the right and duty to the apostolate from their union with Christ the head … they are assigned to the apostolate by the Lord Himself. (*AA* 3)

This was underlined by the last document of the Council, *Gaudium et spes*:

> Lay people should know that it is generally the function of their well-formed Christian conscience to see that the divine law is inscribed in the life of the earthly city; from priests they may look for spiritual light and nourishment. Let the lay people not imagine that their pastors are always such experts, that to every problem which arises, however complicated, they can readily give a concrete solution, or even that such is their mission. Rather, enlightened by Christian wisdom and giving close attention to the teaching authority of the Church, *let the lay people take on their own distinctive role.* (*GS* 43, emphasis added)

Catholic Voices tapped directly into this understanding of the laity.

The birth of a project

In 2010, we chose twenty-five ordinary Catholics and ran a four-month-long training course on the 'neuralgic issues' – where Church and contemporary society clash. Our list of neuralgic issues was inspired, in part, by the list of objections raised by an anti-papal coalition of humanists, secularists and equality activists under the banner of Protest the Pope. Their case was that Pope Benedict XVI should not be accorded the honour of a publicly funded state visit because the position of the Catholic Church on questions such as women, contraception, AIDS, abortion, homosexuality, euthanasia, as well as its attempt to 'interfere' in politics and 'cover up' abuse, were scandalous to modern British susceptibilities. (The list, of course, was easily expanded: the Church's opposition to science, the Vatican's hoarding of money, the 'anti-Semitism' of Pius XII, the fact that the Vatican was not a 'real' state and so on, were also part of the Protest the Pope campaign, but many of these reflected an obviously atheist or secularist bias, and were of less interest to the media.)

In wanting our speakers to be able to explain Catholic thinking on these topics, we realized that having the arguments and being able to express them was in many ways the simpler part. Far harder was instilling the mentality needed for this work.

We wanted our speakers to realize, for example, that 'the media' had no anti-Catholic bias or agenda, but sought to hold people and institutions to account. It was a function the media carried out on behalf of 'society', and was directed at any institution or group that claimed a public role. Their questions might be tough, but so were the questions Catholics get asked in bars or over the dinner table. In seeking balance, the media requires Catholics to explain themselves as well and as clearly as possible, so as to contrast their views with those opposed to the Church. It may seem paradoxical, we explained, but the news media want from us what we also want: the best possible exposition of the story from our side – and therefore we should lose any fear we may have of appearing there.

Of course, there are individuals hostile to the Church in the media, but hostility is also present in government, universities, trade unions or even our own families. But there was no institutional or corporate hostility as such. Rather, the media reflect society. And society – especially educated, urban, liberal Western society, transfixed by the ethic of autonomy – was often scandalized by the Church. Blaming the media, in other words, was at best a distraction from the real event. At worst, it meant excluding yourself from a conversation which might change society's attitudes.

The attitude we wanted to instill was, in fact, the complete reverse. We wanted the speakers to welcome hostility and controversy, because these were opportunities to communicate. The Church, we explained, was a *skandalum*, a stumbling block, to secular modernity. The indignation which the Church aroused was, in this sense, a blessing. When the media turned to us and said: 'how do you justify that?' they were interested; and getting interest, as any communications expert will agree, is half of the battle.

Having persuaded them that the media were not out to get them and that controversy equalled opportunity, the final challenge was to invite the speakers to take advantage of the brief airtime they were given to turn around misconceptions and shed light on the Church's true positions – and to do so in ways that were compelling. To do this, we developed our 'reframing' techniques, which we will describe shortly. And having taught them how to prepare for interviews, we then gave them practice at it – with real radio and TV presenters, hired for the day from the BBC and Sky News – in 'as-live' three-or four-minute interviews on imagined or recent news stories.

After launching to the media – and explaining that we were not the Church's spokespeople, but had the bishops' blessing to explain Catholic positions on neuralgic issues – we were in about 100 news programmes during Pope Benedict's visit to the United Kingdom and in the weeks leading up to it. Catholic Voices became part of the Church chatter on the airwaves, cheerfully explaining why it would not be a good idea to sell the Vatican Museums, or responding to a claim that the Church thought women too stupid to ordain, or showing that the Church's case against euthanasia was a defence of the vulnerable. In dozens of programmes, millions saw and heard a different face to the Church. And in a visit judged overall to have been a great media success for the Church – something that in itself generated great interest across the world because of Britain's famous secularism – Catholic Voices was seen as having made an innovative contribution.

Developing Catholic Voices in the United kingdom and across the world

Soon after the pope left, the bishops of England and Wales told us they were keen for more people to be trained in different parts of the country, in support of their 'Confidently Catholic' agenda. We have done so each year, training around twenty speakers each time on three-weekend courses in Leeds in 2011, Bristol in 2012 and Manchester in 2013. As our team of speakers has expanded, we have managed to grow our media presence. In the papal transition of 2013, for example, beginning with Benedict XVI's resignation and ending with the election of Francis, thirty of our speakers were on almost 200 different news programmes. On the whole, we have managed to clip and upload the interviews, so that the CV website now has quite a large audio and video library.

We realized in 2011 that we needed a means of bringing the CVs together and providing them with ongoing formation. The CV Academy is a monthly gathering, usually with a speaker and Q&A, that tries to reproduce the pace of a radio or TV programme; participants come to get briefed, and then 'try out' different ideas. The focus is on developing a language of the common good. The CV Comment blog complements the Academy, offering analysis and briefings on news related to the Church.

In 2012, a major focus of the Academy was same-sex marriage, the topic that has come second only to the papal visit and papal transition in terms of the number of interviews it has generated. As a result of various Academy sessions, we wrote a briefing paper, 'In Defence of Conjugality: the common-good case against same-sex marriage',[2] which was read by many MPs and used by the Bishops' Conference of New Zealand in preparing their response on the issue. Together with the Coalition for Marriage, Catholic Voices was one of the few civil society organizations speaking against the measure; even though same-sex marriage (SSM) was opposed by the majority of British people, it was so successfully framed as a gay civil rights issue that almost no one was willing to be branded as intolerant by speaking out against it.

Two more UK-based activities of Catholic Voices need a brief mention here also. The first is that we have found ourselves more and more being asked to train dioceses, religious orders, charities and other Church organizations in the techniques for which we have become known – or simply being called on to provide training and consultancy for a particular communications issue. Although Catholic Voices remains independent in the sense that no one tells

---

[2]   The paper can be downloaded online. www.catholicvoices.org.uk. The arguments were developed further in Austen Ivereigh, 'The Destruction of Conjugality', in Anastasia de Waal (ed.), *The Meaning of Matrimony: Debating Same-Sex Marriage* (Civitas, 2013).

us what to say on air, we now recognize that we are offering a service as much to the Church as to the media, to the benefit of both. A second surprising development is public speaking training. Many of our speakers are increasingly asked not just to argue the Church's case in studios, but in parishes and chaplaincies too.

Since 2010, CV has spread to many different countries (currently fifteen), including Ireland, Poland, Spain, Lithuania, Italy, Portugal, the Netherlands, Australia, Canada, the USA, Mexico, Venezuela, Trinidad and Tobago, Chile, and Argentina. We do not initiate the projects but assist groups who, having seen us, contact us wanting to do the same. We ask them first to obtain the blessing of their local bishops, and make clear a few basics: the group should not be the vehicle of a particular agenda or group, should have a positive attitude to the media and should be autonomously financed and organized. Then we assist them in a number of ways, and usually come out to begin their training.

The CV 'method': Reframing

At the heart of the CV project's success are the methods and techniques it has developed for enabling Catholics to be confident and joyful in responding to criticism or misunderstanding, and the way these are used as opportunities to present the Church's life-giving messages. We saw that with our way of communication we had avoided three common dangers often present in other Church communications.

First, we had avoided being angry. It is easy to see why religious people get angry when faced with what are often offensively framed news stories. But a person who gets angry ceases to communicate. An 'us and them' mentality can develop and the impression given to the public can become disagreeable: religious and anti-religious people fighting puts off ordinary people from having anything to do with religion.

The second danger we tried to avoid was being defensive. As Catholics, we felt that our Church did not need defending; on the contrary, it did wonderful things in the world and if some of its members had done wrong we were more than ready to accept it. A related danger is to appeal to our freedom: 'I let you do whatever you like, let us live as Catholics in the way we like.' This is like admitting that what we do has little value but that in the twenty-first century we should be allowed to behave as we like. On the contrary, we hold that what we believe and what we do has great value. That is why we encouraged members of the team to 'tell their story' in the short time available to them in the media, and in such a compelling way that after they finished, people listening to them would say: 'I want that.'

Finally, we sought to avoid the third danger of missing the chance to communicate. A news story is an open door. It may portray the Church in a negative light, but it brings an opportunity to use the microphone. By their nature, news stories about the Church will be based on some element of drama and scandal; waiting for a positive story could mean waiting forever and never communicating. The important thing was to be able to spot a negative frame – an unconscious assumption about the Church – and to know how to step outside it, and show it to be false, while communicating the true picture. It is not just about surviving a storm, but also about dancing in the rain. We will benefit from contact with criticism. As *Gaudium et spes* forty-four points out, 'The Church admits that she has greatly profited and still profits from the antagonism of those who oppose or who persecute her.'

At the heart of our communication strategy was the idea of the 'positive intention': that behind each question and criticism there is always a value, and that most times, even in hostile situations, this value is a Christian value. The 'reframing' of the news stories, therefore, must start by understanding the criticism directed at the Church, finding the positive intention behind the criticism (there may be other intentions also that are not so positive, but these are ignored), agreeing with that intention and starting our response from there. The effect, we saw, was a real engagement between the people on different sides of the argument, and a willingness to listen to each other.

Once, when giving a presentation about Catholic Voices to a group of young people, a nineteen-year-old emailed us later to explain his own take on the 'positive intention'. He described how he had been to an abortion clinic protest and had had a sudden intuition that

> there is actually something in common between us and the nurses and staff running the clinics: we all wanted to help the poor, vulnerable women who were pregnant and confused about what to do. So it is vital not to condemn people, as we are all human and often both have similar values at our core: life, education, protecting the frail and vulnerable.

Other principles we have developed in our work include our basic aim of shedding light rather than heat. So often in these discussions the arguments are so heated that people stop listening. We go to the media to clarify, not to battle, and try to find simple words to explain complex ideas.

Another principle of Catholic Voices is 'witnessing, not winning': we do not see the other side as the enemy but want to speak starting with what is common to us. We want to communicate the message in a positive way, as we understand that the message of the Church is a 'yes' to life, to women, to freedom and to life – despite the fact that it sometimes seems difficult to frame it that way. We always want to be compassionate and human, showing our message by the way we behave in studios.

Our project aims to communicate the Church in a new era, one where information reaches people through news channels, including information about the Church. With knowledge of the media and the surrounding culture, Catholics will feel much more confident in communicating. Our dream is that in a very few years, the sleeping giant of the laity will awake and hundreds of thousands of ordinary Catholics will heed the call to become communicators – and we can speak, at last, of a truly evangelizing Church.

CV and the New Evangelization

After locating Catholic Voices in the Council's vision of lay people exercising their discipleship, we now want to share some insights from our experience in helping what Archbishop Allen Vigneron at the *Great Grace* conference described as the Council's 'main aim'. This is the renewed missionary impulse which has since been formulated by Pope John Paul II and Benedict XVI as a 'New Evangelization', and which Pope Francis has also developed in calling for a 'missionary proclamation' that begins with mercy.[3] Catholic Voices is being

---

[3] 'There is need of Christians who render the mercy of God visible to the men of today, His tenderness for every creature. We all know that the crisis of contemporary humanity is not superficial but profound. Because of this the New Evangelization – while calling to have the courage to go against the current, to be converted from idols to the only true God – cannot but use the language of mercy, made up of gestures and attitudes even before words. In the midst of today's humanity the Church says: Come to Jesus, all you who labor and are heavy laden and you will find rest for your souls (cf. Mt. 11.28-30). Come to Jesus. He alone has the words of eternal life.' Pope Francis' *Address to Plenary Assembly of Pontifical Council for Promoting the New Evangelization* (14 October 2013).

seen as one of the models – or 'new methods', in Fr Robert Barron's phrase – of the New Evangelization.[4]

The word 'new' in that phrase refers not just to the renewal of energies but the new context of a secularized, yet residually Christian, Western modernity – that is, a culture still strongly informed by often unconscious Christian values which have been detached from their proper teleological context. These values, we have discovered, are often behind criticisms hurled against the Church. But embattled Catholics seldom spot this, and so find themselves arguing against Christian values. Understanding this dynamic, and learning to escape it – which we call reframing – and so to open up new ways of communicating with contemporary modernity, is key to what we might call a 'new apologetics' in the service of that New Evangelization.

That expression appears in the conclusions of the October 2012 Synod of Bishops in Rome, which called for 'a new apologetics of Christian thought, that is, a theology of credibility adequate for a new evangelization'. Credibility is the important word here; we are credible when we speak to peoples' concerns, when we understand their anxieties, but also when we can speak to the strong values implicit in their criticisms.

There are countless examples of residual or subconscious Christian values behind criticism of the Church. Compassion for the victim, for example, has been shown by the great Catholic thinker René Girard to be a cultural development directly and uniquely resulting from the Judeo-Christian revelation[5]; yet the contemporary frame now sees the Church – and organized religion generally – as creating victims, rather than standing with them (a frame that explains the often ferociously distorted reporting of the clerical sex abuse crisis).

Or take the French Revolutionary project of liberty and equality which has so marked the modern era. Despite these ideas arising out of a context of shared beliefs about good, and a teleological understanding of a shared,

---

4   Catholic Voices is one of the 'five examples of the new evangelization' discussed by Fr Stephen Wang in his booklet, *The New Evangelisation: What it is and how to do it* (London: Catholic Truth Society, 2013). And it is one of the six 'new methods' discussed by Fr Robert Barron in his documentary and study guide series, *Catholicism: The New Evangelization* (Word on Fire Ministries, 2013).

5   René Girard's theory, beginning with his 'mimetic theory' of desire and ideas about scapegoating and religion, and the culture-changing effect of the Resurrection in awakening sympathy for the victim, are explained in many books including *I See Satan Fall Like Lightning* (Maryknoll, NY: Orbis, 2001) and *The Scapegoat* (Baltimore: Johns Hopkins, 1989).

God-given dignity, the contemporary narrative sees equality and liberty as needing to be wrested and protected from faith and community. The political project which flows from this assumes that one of the tasks of the modern state is the emancipation of individuals, and especially groups which can claim to be victims, from the burden and control of faith and belief. This project is under one of the French Revolutionary banners of equality, which is, of course, a positive value; yet because it has become tied to an ethic of autonomy hostile to institutions, faiths and civil society in general, the drive to equality has become authoritarian and intolerant.

The message which the liberal project gives to people of faith is: we respect or tolerate religion as a personal narrative, a tribal custom, but what you believe should have no influence on our culture or laws; any argument by you to the contrary will be resisted as fundamentalism or bigotry. By a strange paradox, this narrative is usually expressed in terms of universal human rights, which originate in the Jewish and later Christian claim that all human beings are God-created and therefore all human beings as such have subjective natural rights. Yet anyone who asserts the metaphysical basis for this claim is accused of trying to resurrect the Middle Ages.

Moral relativism seems to be the only conclusion entailed by moral pluralism, but few want to go there: so what we have is a subjective, feelings-based doctrine which claims that people should be free to pursue their own happiness as long as they do not hurt anybody else, and politics is reduced to a battleground of sovereign, autonomous wills. Because there is no shared metaphysics of what it means even to be a human being, issues such as abortion, SSM and euthanasia remain unresolved battlegrounds. What is left is a formal ethics of rights rather than a substantive ethics of the good, in which the greatest social virtue is toleration of others' choices and actions, and the alternative to this is parodied as fascist or communist totalitarianism and medieval theocracy.

This is the 'new' context, one very familiar to Australians. But if Catholics feel sometimes embattled and persecuted, it is important to remember that these are family rows. As Brad Gregory's *The Unintended Reformation* shows, the fragmentation of Christian belief and the capture of churches by nation-states led, through wars of religion and so on, to where we are now – and it is worth following the trail, because however much we may feel alienated from our culture, this is the latest act in a drama that is unmistakably that of the Christian West.[6]

Understanding the peculiar nature of this challenge – we are speaking to a culture imbued with subconscious Christian values, yet which uses those values, again unconsciously, to reject formal religion in general and the Church in particular – calls for a new kind of apologetics, one that understands the dynamic underneath this tendency towards a dictatorship of relativism. But this is not just about 'us' persuading 'them': the new apologetics starts closer to home. A wide-ranging survey commissioned by a serious academic department in the United Kingdom in 2013 asked what people believed about major ethical issues such as same-sex marriage and assisted suicide, and broke them down by religion, and then in turn distinguished between nominal adherents of a faith and those who actively participate. To pick out some typical results for Catholics: on same-sex marriage and assisted suicide, among *practising* Catholics more (46 per cent) are in favour of allowing these compared to those who believe (44 per cent) that such issues should be kept illegal.[7]

Does this mean, as headlines were keen to claim, that churchgoing Catholics disagree with the Church's opposition to both? No. As the survey also showed, almost all practising Catholics understand marriage to be between a man and a woman, and a life remains of absolute value even when it is not seen as such. But most of those who agree with the Church on those issues will be unable to explain why the law should reflect this; in other words, they have not heard the common-good arguments made by the Church that show why the law should keep euthanasia illegal and prevent same-sex couples from accessing the institution of marriage. So their Catholic convictions sit alongside a belief they have internalized from culture: that their views are private, relevant only to them, and any attempt to shape our culture according to those principles is an unwarranted 'imposition'.

As long as Catholics believe this, of course, the missionary aim of Vatican II to shape our culture will be frustrated, and it will be impossible to challenge the commodification of human beings, the culture of death, the dethroning of

---

[6] Brad S. Gregory, *The Unintended Reformation: How a Religious Revolution Secularized Society* (Cambridge, MA: Harvard University Press, 2012).

[7] A summary of the findings of the Lancaster University-commissioned YouGov surveys can be found at http://faithdebates.org.uk/wp-content/uploads/2013/09/1368520681_Summary_Press_Releases_WFD2.pdf.

conjugal marriage, the exploitation of migrants or any of the other ills that face us. And such an attitude erodes the credibility of Catholic faith itself, for a faith which is merely a personal narrative cannot be of God.

The new apologetics is unlike the old apologetics in that it sees as its primary audience not Protestants or atheists or communists but those for whom the ethic of autonomy is the prevailing value. That is why the issues we focus on are those where, of course, the Church presents an 'obviously' scandalous obstacle to the icons of that ethic, such as abortion, sexuality and euthanasia. It is where the news stories are, because the producers know where the sparks around the dinner table happen.

So, the new apologetics is not just about developing ways of speaking to a culture of autonomy; it is also about demonstrating, firstly to the faithful, that the Church has answers to the deepest questions of our society, and then equipping the faithful to engage with those questions around the office water cooler. And teaching them, when they engage, how to reframe.

Learning to reframe

The new apologetics understands that, on the whole, people are not listening to the Church, because what the Church is understood to be offering appears not to be new or interesting. But the neuralgic issues are the exception to that rule, because the Church's apparent perversity in these areas makes it, in fact, a source of endless fascination.

The neuralgic issues are where the communication happens or does not happen. It is where people turn to you and say, 'you're a Catholic, aren't you? How do you justify this or that?' The new apologetics is about learning to be in that space, being comfortable in that space; it is about learning to use the short time that that attention gives you to step out of the frames and communicate the truth of the Church's position. If you reinforce the frame, people do not hear you, even if your arguments are elegant and well thought-out; they just switch off.

The reason why is explained and illustrated by Jonathan Haidt's *The Righteous Mind.*[8] Most people are not persuaded by argument, unless the

---

[8] Jonathan Haidt, *The Righteous Mind: Why Good People are Divided by Politics and Religion* (London: Allen Lane, 2012).

argument speaks to their core moral intuition. The core moral intuition of contemporary society is based on the autonomy ethic: no one has the right to impose their view on others. So anyone who appears to take for granted that this view can be imposed will be rejected, whatever their reasons. That is why most Catholics who begin their sentences with 'the Church says …' or 'the Church believes …' do not get very far; they are reinforcing the frame that the Church is seeking to impose its view, or is clinging to its own beliefs in the face of reality, and so on.

There are many other frames: religious belief is irrational, but unbelief requires no explanation; faith has been superseded as a basis for moral belief; institutions such as churches put their own interests before those of society; and so on. Each of us can make our own list. But the point to grasp about a frame is that it is usually unspoken yet speaks louder than any words. And if a Catholic speaks to that frame, reinforcing it, they are not 'heard'.

But the good news is that if you can re-frame – as we teach in our workshops – then you enable the conversation that we need to have. You never get to that conversation if you are not credible. Someone who does not understand the value implicit in criticism of the Church is not credible; they are simply dismissed. A credible apologist is one who can spot that value, affirm it, and then challenge the presuppositions that have detached that value from its source. This is one dimension of 'reading the signs of the times', as Vatican II asks us to do: sifting the elements of modernity, spotting what is ours and affirming it, while challenging other elements which contradict and betray the Gospel.

Our experience in Catholic Voices is that when we recognize the residual Christian value in the criticism of the Church, and we affirm it, we are able to step outside the frame. What follows is at least a conversation, and sometimes a conversion.

Healing divisions

In our experience, now, after three years going around the world to support CV projects as they arise, we are confident that there is a sizeable number of people called to be 'voices' for the Church, happy to receive a little training in reframing and to be supported in working out what to say and how to say it.

Some are priests, but most are lay people. They do this work alongside their current commitments at work and in the home – in fact, it is vital that they do not move from there – and they do so by virtue of their discipleship, not as part of an institutional communications plan.

Pope John XXIII did not mean by *aggiornamento* that the Church should change its teaching to fit modernity, but that the Church should reform in order to be credible in converting culture. The constant mission of the Church to introduce the world to Christ means learning how to speak to the world, to call it into unity with God. That speaking to the world also necessarily changes how we speak and engage. Just as the Greco-Roman culture of the early Church changed when it met other cultures, in the same way, the Church of the Counter-Reformation has had to change to engage with modernity.

George Weigel writes in *Evangelical Catholicism* that under Pope Leo XIII at the end of the nineteenth century, the Church began to abandon that Counter-Reformation model which had defined it so clearly since the sixteenth and seventeenth centuries, and moved towards what he calls 'evangelical Catholicism', a transition finally made possible by the Second Vatican Council. But then the process stalled as the Church turned in on itself in a dispute between liberals and conservatives, which, says Weigel, was essentially an argument about modernity, which Vatican II should have made unnecessary – between those who wanted the Church to adapt to modernity and those who wanted to retreat from it into a fortress. Only with Popes John Paul II, Benedict XVI and now Francis, argues Weigel, has evangelical Catholicism been able to struggle to maturity.[9]

Catholic Voices in the United Kingdom, and wherever else it has been set up has deliberately refused applications from Catholics who are angry with the Church and its leadership, from either wing. Angry people are poor communicators. But above all, angry Catholics, whether liberals or conservatives, are incapable of living in that tense space which evangelical Catholicism calls on us to occupy, neither rejecting modernity nor uncritically embracing it, being in the world, at its margins, but not of it.

That is only possible to do if you are nourished by the Word and sacraments and the deep relationships of trust and support that Catholic community provides;

---

[9]   George Weigel, *Evangelical Catholicism: Deep Reform in the 21st-Century Church* (New York: Civitas Books, 2013).

hence our speakers are not just regular Mass-goers, but also very involved in the life of the Church. That allows us to be diverse. We look for people who care about the just wage, the death penalty and youth unemployment, as well as people who stand up for the unborn and conjugal marriage. We have Catholic Voices of different educational backgrounds, and varied professions and states of life, who vote for different parties and come from different organizations and subcultures within the Church.

The Vatican commentator John Allen cites Catholic Voices as an example of what he calls much-needed 'zones of friendship' within the Church that can overcome the post-conciliar legacy of Catholic tribalism.[10] If we succeed, it must be because our focus is *ad extra, ad gentes*: a Church which learns how to better explain itself to others is by definition more united. One conclusion, then, is that a new apologetics for the New Evangelization is a way not just to advance the primary aim of the Second Vatican Council, but also to transcend the harmful divisions which followed it.

Pope Francis: 'Missionary proclamation'

Pope Francis has dramatically accelerated the New Evangelization with an energetic campaign to put the whole Church on a missionary footing. His remarks on the eve of the conclave, when he contrasted a 'self-referential' Church seeking to live by its own light, as opposed to a missionary Church, which is centred on Christ and present in the 'peripheries' – existential, social – of our society, made a strong impact on the cardinals.

Since his election, that impact has spread, above all to non-believers and alienated Catholics, who are deeply struck by the '*kairos* of mercy' which he has proclaimed. His credibility resides, not least, in his decisive reform of ailing elements of the Vatican Curia, his harsh words against careerism, corruption, clericalism and other symptoms of a 'self-referential' Church, and his public rejection of the trappings of papal monarchy in favour of a 'Church that is poor for the poor'.

---

[10] John Allen, 'Thoughts on post-tribal Catholicism', *National Catholic Reporter* (15 April 2011), http://ncronline.org/blogs/all-things-catholic/thoughts-post-tribal-catholicism.

On the back of that credibility, he has attempted an audacious reframe of the Church's engagement with the modern world, summarized in his observation that 'the proclamation of the saving love of God comes before moral and religious imperatives'.[11] In a number of headline-generating, unscripted interviews – on the papal plane back from Rio, to Brazilian TV, to *Civiltà Cattolica* and the atheist Eugenio Scalfari – Pope Francis has turned heads, both within the Church and outside it, by his commitment to what he calls 'proclamation in a missionary style' which focuses 'on the essentials, on the necessary things … what fascinates and attracts more, what makes the heart burn, as it did for the disciples at Emmaus'. In the same interview with the Jesuit magazine, he said:

> We cannot insist only on issues related to abortion, gay marriage and the use of contraceptive methods. … But when we speak about these issues, we have to talk about them in a context. The teaching of the church, for that matter, is clear and I am a son of the church, but it is not necessary to talk about these issues all the time.

The 'context' here is the love and mercy of God. To speak of truth without showing the love that underpins that truth reinforces the frame of the Church as a curmudgeonly scold. By demonstrating what he calls 'nearness, proximity' – the ability to come alongside people – the pope has reframed the moral truth of what the Church proclaims. 'I see the church as a field hospital after battle,' he says. 'It is useless to ask a seriously injured person if he has high cholesterol and about the level of his blood sugars! You have to heal his wounds. Then we can talk about everything else.'

The wound of gay people, for example, is their exclusion and marginalization, a mistreatment historically justified by moral disapproval of homosexuality: thus Catholic teaching on homosexuality as a 'disordered orientation' has been 'heard' – falsely – as supporting or legitimating the historic mistreatment of gay people. In Catholic Voices we always begin any discussion of a homosexuality-related issue by citing the Church's opposition to that mistreatment. We remind people that the Church in England and Wales in the 1950s backed the Wolfenden Report decriminalizing homosexuality, that

---

[11] Interview with Antonio Spadaro, S. J., of *Civiltà Cattolica*, published in English as 'A Big Heart Open to God' by *America* magazine (www.americamagazine.org) and *Thinking Faith* (www.thinkingfaith.org).

our parish churches have many gay people worshipping in them, and that we believe in the intrinsic dignity of every human being, whatever their race or faith or sexual orientation. Before arguing against same-sex marriage, for example, we need to show that we are committed to the historic pursuit of civil rights for gay people.

On board the papal plane back from Rio, Pope Francis began his answer on the subject by saying:

> If a person is gay and seeks the Lord and has good will, who am I to judge that person? The *Catechism of the Catholic Church* explains this point beautifully but says, wait a moment, how does it say, it says, these persons must never be marginalized and 'they must be integrated into society'.

What Pope Francis gives is straight Catholic teaching, but he has taken the trouble to understand the wound (exclusion) and the positive intention (integration) and has spoken first to these. He is not downplaying Catholic teaching on sexuality, but he wants it to be seen in the context of God's love and mercy, which means the unconditional acceptance and integration of all. He knows that without the reframe, the rest will not be heard.

Against the frame that faith is a set of propositions or ideas, Francis shows that it is primarily about love, mercy and belonging – a *relationship* that spills out into *relationships*. Against the frame that the Church stands in judgement over others, Francis demonstrates – not least every week at the General Audiences – that the Church above all embraces and welcomes. Against the frame of the Church as a 'smug club', Francis offers a Church at the service of the whole of humanity – a battlefield hospital that tends the wounded, open to all and welcoming to all. Against the frame of a pope as a distant monarch, Francis shows – in his spontaneity, informality, directness and lovingness – that the pope is, first of all, a servant and pilgrim.

And against the frame of the Church as a haughty, unchanging institution, weighted down by tradition, Francis calls for the Church, as he said in Assisi, to strip itself of worldliness.[12] Ten days later, in an address to the Pontifical Council for the New Evangelization, the pope repeated the idea, stating that the credibility of Catholic witness requires continued commitment to the evangelical reforms of the Council. 'We must continue on the path of

---

[12] 'Pope in Assisi: Christians must strip themselves of worldliness', Vatican Radio (4 October 2013).

Vatican Council II', he said, 'stripping ourselves of useless and harmful things, of false worldly securities which weigh down the Church and damage her true face.' And he called for the Church to use 'the language of mercy, made up of gestures and attitudes even before words'.[13]

A pope who instinctively reframes is taking the new apologetics in a wholly new direction. The Greek virtue of *parrhesia* – apostolic zeal and courage – will continue to be needed, because Francis does not soften the challenge of the Gospel. But by helping to heal the chasm between the Church and contemporary culture through his proclamation of a *kairos* of mercy, he is opening new paths for every baptized person – every *cristoforo*, or bearer of Christ – to take on our mission to the margins.

---

[13] *Address to Plenary Assembly of Pontifical Council for Promoting the New Evangelization* (14 October 2013).

7

To Awaken the Spirit: Proposing a Vatican II Faith to a Secular World

Mark Coleridge

The title of my chapter, 'To Awaken the Spirit', is all my own work, but the subtitle, 'Proposing a Vatican II Faith to a Secular World', is what I was given. Each element of the subtitle is worth pondering, to see what it actually means. But let me, in topsy-turvy Antipodean style, begin with the last of the three elements, 'a secular world', because the language here is slippery, including as it does terms like 'secularization', 'secularity' and 'secularism'.

In my lexicon, 'secularization' refers to a process the roots of which are in large part biblical. It is first of all a de-sacralization of the natural world which pagan religion, in the past as in the present, always sacralizes. At the heart of this de-sacralization is the Bible's sense of divine transcendence, one implication of which is that God is not tied to any one place, as paganism held. The God of Israel may have been originally a desert God; but ancient Israel eventually came to see that this God was no less sovereign in the fertile land of Canaan than in the wilderness.

Nor was this God only the God of Israel; because after the Exile, when the Babylonian god Marduk seemed to have trumped the God of Israel and should therefore have been worshipped, the Bible solves the theological problem simply by declaring that the God of Israel is the God of all peoples and nations, just as he is the God of all places. Marduk is no god at all.

Political power is also de-sacralized in the Bible. Ancient Israel certainly had kings, but you have only to read chapters 8–12 of 1 Samuel to see what a theological struggle went on before the monarchy was accepted. A king was eventually given to Israel but on strict condition that he be as much subject to the law of God as anyone else in the community. In the surrounding cultures of the ancient Near East, the law was placed on the lips of the king. He was regarded as the one to whom the divine task of ordering the chaos was entrusted, and in Egypt at least the pharaoh was revered explicitly as divine. In ancient Israel, however, the source of the law was not the king but God; even the mediation of the law to the people was entrusted not to the king but to Moses, who functions in scripture as a protean figure designed to put political figures in their proper place. This is what I mean by the Bible's de-sacralization of political power. It is the Bible's way of saying that God alone is God.

All of which is a somewhat long-winded way of saying that what I mean by secularization is by no means all bad. At least that is what God seems to think, if we take the Incarnation to be the secularization of God, which I think it is. In that sense, the Incarnation is the climax of a process of secularization throughout the history of ancient Israel. And just as the Incarnation has a pre-history in the life of ancient Israel, so too it has a post-history in the life of Western cultures, in which de-sacralization and re-sacralization have contended under the influence of various forces, some indebted to the Bible, others more indebted to the Roman Empire.

If secularization refers to a historical process, secularity in my lexicon refers to the character of the cultures produced by such a process. Secularized cultures like Australia have about them a quality of secularity. But secularism is something again. In my understanding, it refers to an ideology, spawned from the process of secularization but significantly more negative in its connotation and more pernicious in its effects. Secularist ideology a priori excludes God, indeed the supernatural, from consideration in a world where the human being is wholly in charge and where reason, understood as the enemy of religion, is the ultimate arbiter. Such ideology may not always reject religion on principle, but it will at least reduce religion to the strictly private domain or to useful works in society like education and health care. As Rowan Williams points out, the paradox is that 'secularism and fundamentalism feed off each other'.[1] They may see themselves as implacable enemies, yet one ideology gives birth to the other.

In speaking of 'a secular world', my theme gathers up these various elements. The secular world that we know and to which we must speak is a world which

---

[1] Rowan Williams, *Faith in the Public Square* (2012), p. 16.

is in part the product of the process of secularization; it has about it a proper secularity. Here I refer to the Augustinian distinction between the sacred, the profane and the secular taken up by Cardinal Francis George of Chicago in an address at the Library of Congress entitled *What Kind of Democracy Leads to Secularism?*[2] The secular, or the *saeculum* as the cardinal also calls it, is the space between the sacred and the profane that respects and safeguards the distinctiveness of each, the space where there can occur conversations between faith and culture on the one hand, and faith and reason on the other. In that sense, secularity is required for the kind of dialogue imagined by my theme: proposing a Vatican II faith to a secular world. Yet the term 'a secular world' also picks up the darker forces of secularist ideology which are also at work in the world to which we must speak.

Before we speak, therefore, we need to make critical judgements about which elements are positive and which negative. An incisive and balanced critique of culture is a vital pre-requisite if we wish to propose a Vatican II faith to a secular world, avoiding the extremes of adulation and antagonism. Such a critique will understand that in any human culture the sacral and the secular intermingle in ways that are at times surprising. Indeed, it could be said that each in some sense contains the other, or at least elements of the other.

Beyond these general considerations, I want now to suggest in more detail the profile of what we call the secular world. Let me name here a number of interrelated features of 'the secular world' as I understand it:

1. A suspicion of authority in individuals and institutions, and a redefinition of authority and its exercise – more demotic, with a demand for accountability and transparency.
2. Individualism, the autonomy of the self (do-it-yourself), with a diminished sense of the common good.
3. Exclusion of or indifference to God and the supernatural, though not uninterested in the spiritual.
4. The sense that human beings are in charge of their own destiny.
5. The turn from the past to the future, from static to dynamic, with dominant myths of progress and evolution.

---

[2] Cardinal Francis George, Address at the Library of Congress, *What Kind of Democracy Leads to Secularism?* (13 February 2007).

6. Historical consciousness and the sense of discontinuity and relativization
   it brings, leading to a rejection of the absolute.
7. Trust in reason and its progeny science and technology, especially cyber-
   technology, not only to better our lives but also to make a better world.
8. Obsession with rights and a penchant for liberation myths, even though
   freedom is paradoxically redefined by genetics and depth-psychology.

The historical roots of such a profile are deep and complex, with culturally
seminal figures like Charles Darwin, Karl Marx and Sigmund Freud and culturally seminal events like the Renaissance, the Reformation and the Enlightenment playing their part. But whatever its provenance and however much
to our taste it may or may not be, this is the world in which we find ourselves
and to which we must propose the Gospel of Jesus Christ.

Yet my theme speaks not of the Gospel of Jesus Christ but of 'a Vatican II faith';
and I turn now to the question of what that might mean. In his speech opening
the Council, Pope John XXIII said that 'the substance of the ancient doctrine
of the deposit of faith is one thing, and the way it is presented is another'.[3] The
Council, he went on to say, must look to the latter while leaving the former
intact. That sounds simple enough, but fifty years later it looks anything but
simple. It touches the large hermeneutical question of the relationship between
form and content; and it seems clear now that in the legacy of the Council the
two have interacted in ways that were not foreseen by the Council or by the
pontiff who convened it. The liturgy is a prime arena in which this appears.

In a series of important studies, John O'Malley has analysed the rhetoric
of Vatican II and shown the complex and powerful interrelationship of form
and content. He claims that the Council made a deliberate decision to 'move
from the dialectic of winning an argument to the dialogue of finding common
ground'.[4] He traces the roots of this decision to the classical rhetorical form of
panegyric, the epideictic genre. He describes the genre in these terms:

> [It is] not so much to clarify concepts as to heighten appreciation for a
> person, an event, an institution, or to evoke emulation of an ideal. Its goal
> is the winning of assent, not the imposition of conformity from outside. Its
> instrument is persuasion, not coercion.[5]

---

[3]   John XXIII, *Opening Address of the Second Vatican Council* (11 October 1962).
[4]   John O'Malley, *What Happened at Vatican II* (Cambridge, MA: Belknap of Harvard, 2008), p. 47.
[5]   John O'Malley, *What Happened at Vatican II*, p. 47.

It is, according to O'Malley, 'a rhetoric of invitation', which is what the Council meant when it used the word 'pastoral' to describe its style. Nothing like this had been seen in conciliar history, where the style had been clearer, more concise, more confrontational, more legislative and juridical.

In his exegesis of the Council's language, O'Malley notes the preponderance of what he calls 'equality-words' (e.g. People of God, brothers and sisters, collegiality), 'reciprocity-words' (e.g. cooperation, partnership, collaboration), 'humility-words' (e.g. pilgrim Church, servant-leadership), 'change-words' (e.g. development, progress, evolution) and 'interiority-words' (e.g. charism, conscience, holiness).[6] O'Malley argues that this linguistic shift generated a new style which was anything but cosmetic:

> [A] style less autocratic and more collaborative, a style willing to seek out and listen to different viewpoints …, a style eager to find common ground with 'the other' ,…, a style committed … to working with persons and institutions outside the Catholic community.[7]

Such a shift in style, O'Malley claims, entailed not an assault on the core of Catholic faith but a shift in 'value-system'.

This shift in 'value-system' meant that the Catholic Church was wanting to adapt to 'the modern world' (to use the Council's own term) not just by using its instruments like technology (as the Vatican had done through the twentieth century) but by making her own the modern world's cultural assumptions and values – not in a way that eroded Catholic faith, but in a way that was more than cosmetic.

Central to this process was the acceptance of contemporary historical consciousness – to the point where Bruno Forte could describe Vatican II as 'the Council of history'.[8] This was the end of the dominance of what Bernard Lonergan has called classicism – the static worldview which meant in his terms that culture was 'conceived not empirically but normatively, not as the meanings and values inherent in a given way of life, but as the right set of meanings and values that were to be accepted and respected if one was not

---

6 Ibid., pp. 49–50.
7 Ibid., pp. 307–8.
8 Ormond Rush, 'Toward a Comprehensive Interpretation of the Council and its Documents', in *Theological Studies* (2012), p. 557.

to be a plebeian, a foreigner, a native, a barbarian.'[9] It was a turn from the metaphysical to the historical. The Council referred to Christ as 'the key, centre and end of all human history', but this did not exclude the dynamic sense of human history that was not unrelated to the Enlightenment's shift from the past to the future.

For the Enlightenment, the turn from the past to the future involved a radical sense of discontinuity with what had gone before. Genuine progress required a genuine break with the past, even if it meant for the French Revolution the beheading of the king and a host of others with him. The bloodshed was the price of progress. It was this which led the Catholic Church to resist so resolutely not only the Revolution but all that flowed from it through 'the long nineteenth century', a term used by some to describe the Catholic Church's history from the French Revolution to the Second Vatican Council. Obviously, the Council did not lurch from the sense of radical continuity upon which the Church had long insisted to the sense of radical discontinuity preferred by the *philosophes* and their heirs, both intellectual and political. What the Council sought was a balance between continuity and discontinuity – though 'discontinuity' is not part of its vocabulary. Nor for that matter is 'change', with terms such as 'progress' and 'development' preferred. As Pope Benedict XVI pointed out more than once, the tension is not between continuity and discontinuity, but between continuity and reform, by which he means organic development rather than rupture.

This question of the relationship between the past, present and future is vital to an understanding of what the Council did. Classicist culture accords unique authority to the past, which is why in earlier times Church reform or reform of elements within the Church was usually thought of as a return to a past when things were thought better not just in the Church but in the world. However, with the rise of historical consciousness and its sense of the radical historicity of human beings and human societies, the past is stripped of much of its authority and the turn is to the future. Hence the dominance of myths of progress and paradigms which draw upon notions of development and evolution and which look to a future better than the past. In order to attain this better future, change is required. Where changelessness was essential to

9   Bernard Lonergan, S. J., 'The Response of the Jesuit, as Priest and Apostle, in the Modern World', in
     Studies in the Spirituality of Jesuits (1970), p. 105.

the classicist view, change is essential to the historicist view. And where earlier Councils had pronounced in ways intended to close the argument, Vatican II was open-ended, more a point of departure than a point of arrival, more the start of a conversation than the end of an argument. For the Council, reform was not a one-off event but an ongoing process.

In its turn to the future, the Council was moderate rather than radical, which is why it spoke not only of *aggiornamento* but also of *ressourcement*. Its logic was the logic of 'back to the future'. *Aggiornamento* and *ressourcement* might seem to move in different directions – one to the past, the other to the present and the future, one resisting history, the other revelling in it. Yet in the end they are part of the same process. The return to the sources was itself a move driven by historical consciousness, a return not just to ancient texts, but to the very 'un-classicist' hermeneutic, rhetoric and theology of those texts, biblical, patristic and liturgical. In the end, *aggiornamento* – slippery term that it is – meant for the Council the retrieval and application to today of the fruits of *ressourcement*.

The acceptance of historical consciousness implied a different sense of the relationship between the Church and the world than was implied by the classicist view. The Church was no longer understood as the perfect society standing above or outside of the flux of history and the challenges of the world. The Church was not an anti-world, not some kind of ghetto. Rather, the Church was seen as herself immersed in history and as an actor within the world with shared responsibility for humanity's future. This meant that the Church and her members were called to work with those outside the Church, 'all people of good will', for the advancement of human society. It also meant that they were to work with other Christians and even people of other religions for the betterment of the world.

Fundamental to the Council's vision was also the turn to the subject. The Gospel must be proclaimed to all people, but it must be done in a way that they can hear and understand. This is the obvious pedagogical principle that any teaching must be adapted to the capacity of its recipients. The Gospel is to be proclaimed in ways that contemporary people find comprehensible and attractive; and it is to be proclaimed not only in the words we speak but also, and perhaps more importantly, in the way we live. This pedagogical principle underlay the Council's choice of its distinctive rhetorical genre and vocabulary.

It is not so much a question of the recipient entering the mentality and idiom of the teacher; rather, it is up to the teacher to communicate in a way adapted to the mentality and idiom of the recipient. This is simple enough to state as a principle, but its implications are vast and its challenges are many.

Long before his election as pope, Joseph Ratzinger wrote that 'the spiritual awakening which the bishops accomplished in full view of the Church, or rather accomplished *as* the Church, was the great and irrevocable event of the Council'.[10] This is a remarkable claim and it leads one to ask about the nature of the spiritual awakening. It seems to me that what the bishops awakened to at the Council was the fact that the truth of all truths, the revelation of all revelations, is God's loving and saving *self*-communication to the world in Jesus and through the Holy Spirit – not a list of abstract truths or a philosophical system, not a moral code or a set of values, not an ideological package or a political programme, but God's total gift of himself.

This spiritual awakening prompted a historical awakening, as the Council understood more deeply the immersion of God in time. It also became a cultural awakening, as the Council came to understand more deeply the personal and cultural factors that affect reception of the Gospel and the truth that God is as much immersed in human cultures as he is in time. This cultural awakening also became a global awakening, as the Council came to understand more deeply that, with the end of colonialism, a Eurocentric Church was giving way to a global Church and that God's will was to communicate not just with the Church but with the world.

Into these awakenings the Council Fathers sought to draw the whole Church; and through the Church they also sought to draw the whole world. This seems to me now the far horizon of Vatican II – in the broad and deep sense, a spiritual awakening of humanity in response to the spiritual numbness that the two world wars left in their wake.

If this is the goal of 'a Vatican II faith', what is its profile? 'Vatican II faith', as I understand it, is an acceptance of God's self-communication to the world in Jesus and through the Holy Spirit. It is an acceptance of the Church as the sacrament of salvation through which this self-communication passes. It is an acceptance that all in the Church are called to holiness and mission, one for

---

[10] Ormond Rush, 'Toward a Comprehensive Interpretation of the Council and its Documents', in *Theological Studies* (2012), p. 552.

the sake of the other. It is an acceptance of history and cultures. It understands the need for change of the right kind. It seeks dialogue with all people of good will rather than confrontation with those who do not see things as we do. It is prepared to listen to and even learn from 'the modern world'. It has an enduring sense of shared humanity with all people, and it looks to a final union with God which is the goal of God's self-communication to the world.

Given what I have said about 'the secular world' and 'a Vatican II faith', what might be said about proposing one to the other? The word 'propose' is itself worth pondering. This is not the kind of language one would find in earlier Councils, but it is very much in the semantic field of Vatican II. It is often said that our task now is to propose rather than impose the appeal of the Gospel, since it would be nonsense to speak of imposing the loving self-communication of God. Laws, demands and constrictions of various kinds might be imposed, but not a loving self-communication. What God offers cannot be imposed from the outside; it can only be accepted from within – again the Council's language of interiority – after it has been proposed from the outside by one who awaits assent and respects freedom.

But it needs to be proposed in a way that is attuned to the mode of reception of those addressed. This means that we have to do all we can to understand a culture in which things are often not what they seem. The liberations promised in the culture are not what they claim to be; but nor is the secularity of the culture quite as godless or as resistant to genuine spirituality as it may seem. Things are both better and worse than they appear to be and we need to see both. Genuine knowledge of the culture is a sine qua non of proclaiming the Gospel now. That will mean knowledge and acceptance of at least three things – historical consciousness, the importance of reason (and its offspring, science and technology) and the culture of human rights and freedom more broadly. All of these will need to be carefully critiqued, but they are non-negotiable in the proposing of faith today.

The turn from the past to the future is another non-negotiable aspect of contemporary secular culture; but at least for the Church, this does not mean an abandonment of the past. It means rather the logic of reform, the logic of 'back to the future', never forgetting the past but not imprisoned by it either. To strike that kind of balance may be one of the more valuable services the Church can render humanity as we work to build the future.

Another sine qua non is the sense of communion that arises from the sense of shared humanity. Communion is a word which we tend to use of the Church these days, but it is also a word which the Council encourages us to use of other Christians and other religious people of whatever stamp; in the end, it is a word which the Council encourages us to use of all humanity. At this point, we cannot afford to be naïve: there are some who loathe us with a visceral hatred. We have to live with that as best we can, as Christians have always done. But there are many others who are not hostile; more likely they are indifferent. If we can find the right words, images and gestures, then they are willing to look and listen. One thinks of Pope Francis and the interest he has stirred beyond the bounds of the Catholic community; and John XXIII is an even more obvious case in point.

Most important of all in some ways is the capacity not to propose an impersonal message but to present to the secular world the face of Christ himself, to lead people to the person of Jesus crucified and risen, the encounter with whom is the heart of Christianity and therefore of a Vatican II faith. In *Novo Millennio Ineunte*, which draws on Vatican II in many ways, Pope John Paul II said that if he were asked what the greatest legacy of the Jubilee celebrations was, he would say without hesitation, the contemplation of the face of Christ. The secular world must be led to know and love Jesus, in whom the self-communication of God is found in its fullness. To encounter him is to experience God as he is, and it is the experience of God rather than words about God that people seek today, and they seek that experience as individuals who themselves have a name and a face. That is why a person-to-person approach seems essential. If the inhabitants of the secular world will not come to us, then we have to go to them, contact them personally, so that our personal contact with them may open them to a personal relationship with Christ. This may sound more evangelical than Catholic, but I think it is true that the Council brought to birth a kind of evangelical Catholicism.

In his opening speech at the Council, John XXIII spoke of the need for the Council to supply 'the medicine of mercy' rather than severity; and this is surely as true now as it was in the shadow of the world wars. The medicine of mercy does not mean that we fail to name sin, but it does mean that we preach and practice limitless forgiveness in an often merciless world. I might add in passing that, for all the summons of the pope and of the Council as a whole, the sacrament of penance, or better the sacrament of mercy, has in the years since the Council entered into a period of crisis. There are various reasons for this, and we may need yet again to revisit the way in which the sacrament is celebrated. But a creative and powerful retrieval of the sacrament may well be an important part of proposing 'the medicine of mercy' to a secular world.

This relates to another essential element in proposing faith to a secular world, and that is a commitment to social justice and an engagement with the poor and the marginalized. This commitment needs to be genuinely religious, indeed Christian, in its motivation, drawing its inspiration from Matthew 25 rather than from political or ideological sources. It also involves a sense of giving to the poor and the marginalized what is their right rather than doing them a favour. It includes advocacy on their behalf in the arenas of decision-making and a will to work for change in economic structures that institutionalize poverty.

A final point I would make concerns Australia in particular, though it may also apply elsewhere. I doubt that it is possible in a culture like this to propose a Vatican II faith, or any faith for that matter, without at least a touch of humour. To put it bluntly, religion without humour just does not sell in Australia. The kind of humour I mean is self-deprecating, not taking ourselves too seriously. It is also ironic, playing on the difference between what seems to be and what is. This is the kind of humour found in the Bible, which is rarely funny in a 'laugh-out-loud' way but which is suffused with a sly irony and in that sense is genuinely humourous.

I conclude by repeating that we need to propose faith not just in words but in the way we live. Some time ago, I read a book by the Queenslander James Cowan. It was a book about St Antony of Egypt, one of the giants of Christian history and a figure who, for reasons I myself find puzzling, has fascinated, even haunted me through the years. Cowan is no conventional believer, but he is a spiritual searcher of a kind not unknown in the secular world. The book recounts his search for the truth of Antony, following his footsteps in Egypt.

There are many memorable observations in the book, but one that leapt off the page at me was at the very end. Cowan writes that people have grown weary of Christianity understood and experienced as 'an entrenched moralism' stripped of 'poetry and extreme life', the kind of 'poetry and extreme life' he rightly finds in Antony and which we recognize supremely in Christ crucified and risen. Rowan Williams speaks of 'the risks of religion's failure to be "religious" enough, religion's poetic inadequacy, its secularism' and this is what Cowan means.[11] It also brings to mind another of Williams' claims, that faith cannot engage secularism by yielding to its assumptions and demands. Faith needs to engage, but on the basis of its own more mysterious assumptions and demands.

If we wish to propose a Vatican II faith to a secular world – and there is no more pressing task at a time when the Church as a whole must become more missionary – then we will need more than a touch of 'poetry and extreme life'. St Antony was one of those figures in the Church – like St Benedict and St Francis – who brought to birth not only a new way of being Christian but a new form of human consciousness and eventually a new civilization. Perhaps, if we are really to propose the Gospel to a secular world, we may need a new Antony, a new Benedict or a new Francis – not for the words they speak but for the witness they give and for the way in which they awaken the human spirit and call forth the Spirit of God.

---

[11] Rowan Williams, *Faith in the Public Square* (London: Bloomsbury, 2012), p. 21.

8

Conclusion: Knowing and Loving the Church after Vatican II

Peter Comensoli

For anyone born after 11 October 1962, access to life in the Church as it was prior to the Second Vatican Council cannot come via experience of it. The same goes for those who were not participants in the heady times during and following the Council; knowledge of that period can only be accessed via the stories and memories of those who lived through it. For these people – now the majority of Catholics in the world – the pre-conciliar Church is not knowable affectively but only intellectually.

Yet, our sainted Pope John Paul II – himself a Council Father – insisted on calling Vatican II 'the great grace bestowed on the Church in the 20th century: there we find a sure compass by which to take our bearings in the century now beginning'.[1] This appreciation of the life-giving gift of the Council was very much evident during the three days of the conference, the *Great Grace*, held in 2013, which sought to honour the insights of St John Paul by adopting his phrase for its theme.

Complementing the lofty vision of our keynote presenters was a lively buzz of conversations and reminisces, discussions and debates among conference participants during the breaks and in the workshops. Particularly noteworthy were the many informal engagements between those who had lived through the Council – a few of whom were eye witnesses – and those, like myself, who have only known the Council through its sixteen teaching documents; in other words, a mingling of the affective and the intellectual. Vatican II was certainly not seen as old news from a bygone era, but a powerful and life-giving river of grace flowing through the Church in Australia of the twenty-first century.

---

[1] John Paul II, *Novo Millennio Ineunte*, p. 57.

What is it about the Second Vatican Council that it remains, fifty years after the event, a source of life-giving grace to a new generation of Christian believers? How can sixteen historically conditioned texts continue to nourish people who never had the experience – and can never have access to the experience – of the Council itself? The image of another river might offer a way towards answering these questions.

The Prophet Ezekiel recounts a vision of a stream flowing from the temple of the Lord, which gradually gathers volume and power until it becomes a river too large to cross (Ez 47.1-12). In this biblical vision, the angel speaks to Ezekiel of the power of the river to produce life: 'Wherever the river goes, every living creature that swarms will live. … And on the banks, on both sides of the river, there will grow all kinds of trees for food … because the water for them flows from the sanctuary' (vv. 9, 12).

It is not simply the volume of water being produced by the river that brings forth life, but the source of that water, the sanctuary of the Lord. The message of the angel is clear: from the Lord comes grace; from Him comes life. And this same sanctuary of the Lord – no longer a vision, but now made flesh in the Incarnation – continues to gush forth with the water of life, mixed with blood, flowing from Christ's opened side (Jn 19.34). The life-giving river of grace, therefore, will always be available to those who seek out its source.

This is where the patrimony of the Council is to find its power to generate a life-giving river of grace for the life of the Church now and into the future; not in the power of the words of sixteen documents *as* documents, but in the life of the one they refer to, Jesus Christ. It is a clear reminder that none of the specific pronouncements of the Church over the millennia – her teachings, order, discipline – will be anything other than exercises in intellectual prowess unless the person of Jesus Christ, abiding in the Catholic Church, is the true source and object of that output. It is only in the Body of Christ that words and texts can then generate life and grace; where the mind can give over to the heart and the intellect is united with the experience of grace.

It is because of this that the Council is both a rich source of energy for the Church and carries its own contingency. At heart (and from the heart), the Council cannot be anything other than a thing of intellectual curiosity unless it is bound to the living tradition of the Church. It is not, therefore, unmoored from what lives, but is life-giving because it is contingent on this rich tradition. For those who come to the words of the Council without sourcing those words in the river of grace flowing from the side of Christ, nothing will be achieved other than an intellectual engagement with a concept. This might be interesting or even fascinating, but that is not the same as life-giving.

The same goes for the words in this book, and all other words about the words of the Council. The various chapters comprising this edited collection, including these concluding remarks, are themselves to be measured according to the extent that they are sourced from the living Word of God. They will take us further into the meaning of the conciliar teachings to the extent that they form a genuine part of the flow of the river of grace. They will be of future value if they are configured to the person at the heart of the Council, not to conceptual images of the Council. The Second Vatican Council can only be properly understood and embraced when it is read from the heart of Christ.

For this reason, purely intellectual engagements with Vatican II will only end up producing fruitless ideologies. Knowing all about Vatican II, and making intellectual judgements of its teachings, themes and outcomes, will not get us to the living Body of Christ. A judgement of radical change resulting from the Council may be proposed as an intellectual exercise – we need only look at the various differences between pre- and post-conciliar teaching and practice to affirm such a possibility – but it cannot generate life in the Church. Likewise, a judgement of rejection of the profound change resulting from Vatican II – hankering instead for a 'purer' ecclesiology and liturgical style based on abstracted, ahistorical and insulated pre-conciliar appearances – will suck life from the Church. One tends towards uncritical accommodation of the world (secularism), the other towards a radical rejection of the world (clericalism). Each turns the Church into a museum; an intellectual curiosity, but no longer a living reality. In our hearts we do not hunger for artefacts but for a living body of truth and love.

Both of these intellectualized judgements of Vatican II are bedfellows of a hermeneutic of rupture. They are sterile seeds that might produce a single crop, but fail to generate any ongoing life able to sustain Christian discipleship. Hermeneutics of rupture, whatever form they take, inevitably prove to be barren.

A hermeneutic is more than simply an interpretation on a particular matter; it is a way of measuring everything – a worldview. A hermeneutic of rupture will break apart that which went before from that which has come about so that the two parts can be independently weighed and judged as generic wholes. In the two examples just highlighted, the hermeneutic of rupture applied to the Second Vatican Council will inevitably lead to either a rejection of the life of the Church as it once was or a rejection of the life of the Church as it now is.

While this reading of a hermeneutic of rupture may seem a little exaggerated, there are certainly streams of thought among some Catholics which seek to push the life of the Church in one of either of these two directions. Both aim for a dividing of the Church into a camp of true believers and a camp of all the rest; both are forms of practical gnosticism. The deep flaw in any form of a hermeneutic of rupture is that it vitiates human history, and therefore the redemptive role of Christ in it. It cannot be a true hermeneutic 'of the Church' because the Church herself is inseparable from salvation history.

But if not 'rupture', then what does a life-giving hermeneutic of the Council look like? Benedict XVI, now pope emeritus, was the last pontiff of the Church to have personally participated in the Council. As historians have noted, his role in shaping key texts of the Council was significant. Consequently, Benedict offers a unique insider perspective on what the Council set out to do.

In 2005 (at the time of the 40th anniversary of the Council's conclusion), Benedict had this to say about the problems that arose as a result of interpreting the Council, and the need to uncover the true meaning of the Council from the perspective of 'reform':

> The hermeneutic of discontinuity is countered by the hermeneutic of reform, as it was presented first by Pope John XXIII in his Speech inaugurating the Council on 11 October 1962. ... It is clear that this commitment to expressing a specific truth in a new way demands new thinking on this truth and a new and vital relationship with it; it is also clear that new words can only develop if they come from an informed understanding of the truth expressed.[2]

Notice how Benedict points out that the effective development of 'new ways', 'new thinking' and 'new words' came about only by a thorough commitment to and understanding of what had already been established as true. The commitment of the Council was to the reform of the Church; but the means through which this was undertaken was to be the growth of new branches

---

[2]   Benedict XVI, *Address to Roman Curia* (2005).

from the trunk of the Christian tradition. What Benedict is expressing here is the principle of catholicity, the internal process of ensuring that the Christian tradition remains both faithful to its roots and fruitful for the world at any given time.

Consider, for example, where the chief conciliar reforms in liturgy, scripture and ecclesiology emerged from. Each of these areas underwent major internal renewal in the period between Vatican I and Vatican II, precipitated by the contemporary circumstances, but undertaken from a principle of a return to the sources, or '*ressourcement*'. When the Council sought a new language through which these areas of Church life would continue to bear fruit, *ressourcement* had already done the work. These examples of conciliar reform have led to major and positive developments in the way the Church worships, in ecumenical and interfaith relations, and in the vocation of the laity in the mission of the Church.

The elements of Benedict's 'hermeneutic of reform' are nothing new in the life of the Church. Both Yves Congar in the 1960s and John Henry Newman in the late 1800s made exactly the same arguments for genuine reform: the application of a principle of internal *ressourcement* as the only way to a true expression of catholicity.

First, Congar:

> There are only two possible ways of bringing about renewal or updating. You can either make the new element that you want to put forward normative, or you can take as normative the existing reality that needs to be updated or renewed. … You will end up with either a mechanical updating in danger of becoming both a novelty and a schismatic reform, on the one hand, or a genuine renewal (a true development) that is a reform in and of the Church, on the other hand.[3]

Secondly, Newman:

> Those [developments] which do but contradict and reverse the course of doctrine which has been developed before them, and out of which they spring, are certainly corrupt; for a corruption is a development in that very stage in which it ceases to illustrate, and begins to disturb, the acquisitions gained in its previous history.[4]

---

[3] Congar, *True and False Reform in the Church*, p. 292.
[4] Newman, *An Essay on the Development of Christian Doctrine*, section 6; note 6, p. 199.

It should not be seen as a mere coincidence that both Newman and Congar are universally recognized as being two of the great 'prophets' who shaped the reforming agenda taken up by the Second Vatican Council. Any analysis of the reception of the Council in the life of the Church today, any contemporary call for reform in the life of the Church precipitated by current events and times, and any future reform proposed, would do well to keep in mind the elements by which genuine ecclesial reform will happen. As a theological friend from outside of the Catholic tradition has remarked: 'No one who has not learned to be traditional can dare to innovate.'[5]

As the saying goes: *Ecclesia semper reformanda est*. But what shape does reform in the life of the Church need to take – locally and globally, individually and collectively – for it to become effective and fruitful? How does the Church go about learning well the way of ongoing reform? Reform is often seen as a 'root and branch' kind of thing: locate the roots, and the branches will follow. For corporations, reform will need to be couched in economic terms; for civic authorities, in bureaucratic terms. While the Church has both corporate and civic dimensions to it, in essence, it is neither of these. Consequently, the kind of reform that the Church needs to undertake has to be particular to its essentially ecclesial reality.

In other words, each reality calls for a response that is particular to its identity and structure. This is because the sources for reform will be found from within, even when the need for reform is recognized from without. Otherwise, there will be no genuine effort to foster a culture of reform, no real movement towards the good. In other words, imposing change from without is not the same as undertaking reform from within. Change can be imposed but need not be causally related to identity and structure. Consequently, it can be ill-fitting and later abandoned. Reform, on the other hand, when based on the principle of internal *ressourcement*, will always have a better chance of taking hold.

For the Church, the principle of reform particular to its identity and structure has its biblical roots in the theological notion of conversion. The Prophecy of Isaiah, for example, begins with – and is based on – the call to conversion of heart. The Lord's Chosen People had rebelled against truth and goodness; their practices and their very lives had become corrupt. The Lord,

---

[5] Oliver O'Donovan, *A Conversation Waiting to Begin*, p. 108.

through Isaiah, calls them back to himself and back to their status as God's chosen:

> Wash yourselves; make yourselves clean; remove the evil of your deeds from before my eyes; cease to do evil, learn to do good; seek justice, correct oppression; bring justice to the fatherless, plead the widow's cause. (Isa. 1.16-17)

The Lord's call to conversion takes the form of a twofold command. The first part is: *cease to do evil*. A decisive break with the past is required, so as to make a start on the road to transformation. An immediate end to evil behaviour by individuals, along with any cultural practices that have become corrupt, is the first step on the road to reform. Genuine repentance of failings and corruption form the basis from which the Church begins the journey of reform. Here are her roots.

On its own, however, the cessation of evil is not enough. A more radical step is required by the Lord to bring about a lasting culture of conversion: *learn to do good*. This second half of the commandment is future oriented. The task of transformation is never finished; the work of reform is ongoing. Conversion is neither a static thing, nor a once-and-for-all, one-off occurrence. While it has an identifiable beginning, it has no fixed conclusion. Conversion is a way of life lived 'in the Lord', who is the source and summit of all that is good.

If genuine reform in the Church can occur only if it is based on a principle of internal *ressourcement* particular to her ecclesial identity and structure, then how is the Church to go about doing this? This is not a question of changing things that need immediate rectification (the first part of the call to conversion), but the deeper and more challenging question of what constitutes effective and lasting cultural transformation in the life of the Church.

The Second Vatican Council itself provided an excellent means of doing this, one which comes from the heart of Christ. As the Council Fathers taught:

> All the faithful of Christ whatever rank or status, are called to the fullness of the Christian life and to the perfection of charity; by this holiness as such a more human manner of living is promoted in this earthly society. In order that the faithful may reach this perfection, they must use their strength accordingly as they have received it, as a gift from Christ.[6]

---

[6] Catholic Church, *Lumen Gentium*, p. 40.

The Council Fathers placed this universal call to holiness at the centre of the Church's self-understanding. To participate in the life of the Body of Christ is to answer the call of the Triune God to take the path of sanctity. The biblical call to conversion – now expressed ecclesially in the call to the ongoing reform of the Church – is summed up in this one call to holiness. From the intellectual expression of a historically conditioned text can be seen the living face of Christ himself: from the Council, through tradition, to source; from knowing to loving. Herein lies the way in which the Council of the past now reaches out to the present, and will be a sure compass into the future.

The Second Vatican Council has shown itself to be a path from knowing to loving the Church, and will be for generations of Christians to come. And more than a path, it is a way – a pilgrimage – into that great stream that becomes a river of living water. Truly, it is a great grace.

Bibliography

Afanassieff, Nicolas, *L'Église du Saint-Esprit* (Paris: Cerf, 1975).

Alberigo, Giuseppi, 'Transition to a New Age', in Giuseppe Alberigo (ed.), *History of Vatican II* (English edn, ed. Joseph A. Komonchak; trans. Matthew J. O'Connell; vol. 5; Maryknoll: Orbis; Leuven: Peeters, 2006), p. 629.

Allen, John, 'Thoughts on post-tribal Catholicism', *National Catholic Reporter* (15 April 2011), http://ncronline.org/blogs/all-things-catholic/thoughts-post-tribal-catholicism.

Barron, Robert, *Catholicism: The New Evangelization* (Word on Fire Ministries, 2013).

Barron, Robert, *The Priority of Christ: Toward a Post-Liberal Catholicism* (Grand Rapids: Brazos Press, 2007).

Barth, Karl, *Ad Limina Apostolorum* (trans. K. R. Crim; Edinburgh: St. Andrew's Press, 1969).

Benedict XVI, *Address to the clergy of Rome* (14 February 2013).

Benedict XVI, Address to the Pastoral Convention on the theme 'Church Membership and Pastoral Co-responsibility' (26 May 2009), http://www.vatican.va/holy_father/benedict_xvi/speeches/2009/may/documents/hf_ben-xvi_spe_20090526_convegno-diocesi-rm_en.html.

Benedict XVI, *Address to the Roman Curia on the occasion of the traditional exchange of Christmas greetings* (22 December 2005).

Bevans, Stephen, 'The Mission Has a Church, the Mission Has Ministers: Thinking Missiologically about Ministry and the Shortage of Priests', *Compass: A Review of Topical Theology* 43.3 (2009), pp. 3–14.

Candler, Peter, *Theology, Rhetoric, Manuduction, or Reading Scripture Together on the Path to God* (Grand Rapids: Eerdmans, 2006).

Catholic Church, *Catechism of the Catholic Church* (London: Burns & Oates, 1994).

Catholic Church, *Lumen Gentium: Dogmatic Constitution on the Church* (1964), http://www.vatican.va/archive/hist_councils/ii_vatican_council/documents/vat-ii_const_19641121_lumen-gentium_en.html.

Chesterton, G. K., *Orthodoxy: The Romance of Faith* (Garden City, NY: Doubleday Books, 1959).

Code of Canon Law (1917), *Codex Iuris Canonici Pii X Pontificis Maximi, iussu digestus, Benedicti Papae XV, auctoritate promulgates*.

Code of Canon Law (1983), http://www.vatican.va/archive/ENG1104/__PU.HTM.

Coleridge, Mark, ABC Radio National, *Encounter*, 'Where is the Fire of Pentecost: Sexual Abuse, the Catholic Church and Culture' (23 May 2010).

Congar, Yves, *Achieving Christian Maturity* (trans. Eileen Kane; Dublin/Melbourne: Gill, 1966).

Congar, Yves, *Lay People in the Church: A Study for a Theology of Laity* (trans. Donald Attwater; London: Bloomsbury, 1957).

Congar, Yves, 'Pneumatology Today', *American Ecclesiastical Review* 167 (1973), pp. 435–49 (443).

Congar, Yves, *The Role of the Laity in the Church* (trans. John R. Gilbert and James W. Moudry; Cork: Mercer, 1955).

Congar, Yves, *True and False Reform in the Church* (trans. Paul Philebert OP; Minnesota: Liturgical Press, 2011), p. 292.

Congregation for the Doctrine of the Faith, *Communionis Notio* [Letter to the Bishops of the Catholic Church on Some Aspects of the Church Understood as Communion], 28 May 1992.

de Mattei, Roberto, *The Second Vatican Council* (*An Unwritten Story*) (trans. Patrick T. Brannan et al; English edn; Fitzwilliam, NH: Loreto, 2012).

De Mey, Peter, 'Church Renewal and Reform in the Documents of Vatican II: History, Theology, Terminology', *The Jurist* 71 (2011), pp. 369–400.

Di Noia, Augustine, 'American Catholic Theology at Century's End: Postconciliar, Postmodern and Post Thomistic', *The Thomist* 54 (1990), pp. 499–518.

Doyle, Dennis M., *Communion Ecclesiology: Vision and Versions* (Maryknoll, NY: Orbis Books, 2000).

Dulles, Avery, 'Can the Word "Laity" Be Defined?' *Origins* 18.29 (29 December 1988), pp. 470–75.

Dulles, Avery, 'The Mission of the Laity', L. J. McGinley Lecture, Fordham University (29 March 2006), http://old.usccb.org/laity/laymin/CardinalDulles.pdf.

Edwards, Gareth, 'Modern English in the Mass', *America* 22 (October 1966), pp. 483–86.

Edwards, Verity, 'Nuns a vanishing breed as few heed calling', *The Australian* (1 April 2013).

Faggioli, Massimo, 'Between Documents and Spirit: The Case of "the New Catholic Movements"', in Heft and O'Malley (eds.), *After Vatican II*, pp. 1–22.

Faggioli, Massimo, '*Sacrosanctum Concilium* and the Meaning of Vatican II', *Theological Studies* 71 (2010), pp. 437–52.

Finucane, Daniel J., *Sensus Fidelium: The Use of a Concept in the Post-Vatican II Era* (San Francisco: International Scholars Publications, 1996).

Francis, *Address to General Assembly of the Italian Bishops' Conference* (24 May 2013), http://en.radiovaticana.va/storico/2013/05/24/total_love_for_jesus_is_the_measure_of_a_man_of_god,_pope_tell/in2-695261.

Francis, 'Address to Leadership of the Council of Bishops' Conferences of Latin America and the Caribbean' (29 July 2013), http://en.radiovaticana.va/news/2013/07/29/pope_francis:_address_to_celam_leadership/in2-714915.

Francis, *Address to Plenary Assembly of Pontifical Council for Promoting the New Evangelization* (14 October 2013).

Francis, *Address to Pontifical Ecclesiastical Academy* (6 June 2013), http://en.radiovaticana.va/news/2013/06/06/pope_to_future_diplomats:_careerism_is_leprosy!/in2-699076.

Francis, *Address to the Bishops of Brazil* (28 July 2013), http://en.radiovaticana.va/news/2013/07/28/pope_francis_to_brazilian_bishops:_are_we_still_a_church_capable_of/in2–714616.

Francis, *Homily on the occasion of the 86th birthday of Benedict XVI, Pope Emeritus* (16 April 2013), http://en.radiovaticana.va/news/2013/04/16/pope:_2nd_vatican_council,_work_of_holy_spirit_but_some_want_to_tur/en1-683419.

Francis, Interview with Antonio Spadaro S. J., of *Civiltà Cattolica*, published in English as 'A Big Heart Open to God' by *America* magazine (www.americamagazine.org) and *Thinking Faith* (www.thinkingfaith.org).

Francis, Letter to Plenary Assembly for Bishops of Argentina (25 March 2013), http://en.radiovaticana.va/news/2013/04/18/do_not_be_afraid_to_go_out_%E2%80%98into_the_deep%E2%80%99,_pope_to_argentine_bishops/in2-684297.

Francis, Pope Francis interviewed by Fr Antonio Spadaro S. J. (ed.) of *La Civiltá Cattolica*, *America Magazine* (30 September 2013).

Francis, 'Pope in Assisi: Christians must strip themselves of worldliness', Vatican Radio (4 October 2013).

Freedman, Samuel, 'A Long Road from "Come by Here" to Kumbaya', *New York Times* (20 November 2010).

Gilson, Étienne, *Letters to Henri de Lubac* (trans. M. E. Hamilton; San Francisco: Ignatius, 1988).

Girard, René, *I See Satan Fall Like Lightning* (trans. James G. Williams; Maryknoll: Orbis, 2001).

Girard, René, *The Scapegoat* (trans. Yvonne Freccero; Baltimore: Johns Hopkins University Press, 1989).

Gray, John, *Liberalism* (London: Open University Press, 1986).

Gregory, Brad S., *The Unintended Reformation: How a Religious Revolution Secularized Society* (Cambridge, MA: Harvard University Press, 2012).

Gregory Nazianzus, Epistle 130, 'Ad Procopium', cited by Joseph Ratzinger, *Principles of Catholic Theology* (San Francisco: Ignatius, 1987).

Grootaers, Jan, 'The Drama Continues Between the Acts: The "Second Preparation" and its Opponents', in Giuseppe Alberigo (ed.), *History of Vatican II* (English edn, ed. Joseph A. Komonchak; vol. 2, Maryknoll, NY: Orbis; Leuven: Peeters, 2003).

Guardini, Romano, *The End of the Modern World* (London: Sheed & Ward, 1957).

Haidt, Jonathan, *The Righteous Mind: Why Good People are Divided by Politics and Religion* (London: Allen Lane 2012).

Havel, Vaclav, 'Politics and Conscience', *Salisbury Review* (January 1985).

Hebblethwaite, Peter, *Paul VI: The First Modern Pope* (Mahweh, NJ: Paulist Press, 1993).

Heft, James L. with John O'Malley (eds.), *After Vatican II: Trajectories and Hermeneutics* (Grand Rapids Michigan: Eerdmans, 2012).

Hoge, Dean R. and Jacqueline E. Wenger, *Evolving Visions of the Priesthood: Changes from Vatican II to the Turn of the New Century* (Collegeville, MN: Liturgical Press, 2003).

Hünnermann, Peter and B. Jochen Hilberath, *Herder theologischer Kommentar zum zweiten Vatikanischen Konzil* (5 vols; Freiburg i/Br: Herder, 2004–06).

Hunt, Anne, 'The Trinitarian Depths of Vatican II', *Theological Studies* 74 (2013), pp. 3–19.

Ignatius of Antioch, 'Letter to the Magnesians; to the Trallians; and to the Smyrnaeans', in *The Epistles* (trans. John Behr; New York: St Vladimir's Seminary Press, 2013).

Ignatius of Antioch, *Letter to the Romans, The Epistles of St. Clement of Rome and St. Ignatius of Antioch* (trans. James A. Kleist; Ancient Christian Writers, vol. 1; New York/Mahwah: Paulist Press, 1946).

International Theological Commission (2007), 'The Hope of Salvation for Infants who die without being Baptised'.

Ivereigh, Austen, 'The Destruction of Conjugality', in Anastasia de Waal (ed.), *The Meaning of Matrimony: Debating Same-Sex Marriage* (Civitas, 2013).

John XXIII, *Acta apostolicae sedis* 54 (1962).

John XXIII, Address on the occasion of the solemn opening of the most holy Council, 11 October 1962, in W. M. Abbott S. J. (ed.), *The Documents of Vatican II* (1966).

John Paul II, *Christifideles Laici* (1988).

John Paul II, *Novo Millennio Ineunte* (2001), http://www.vatican.va/holy_father/john_paul_ii/apost_letters/documents/hf_jp-ii_apl_20010106_novo-millennio-ineunte_en.html.

John Paul II, Apostolic Constitution, *Sacrae Disciplinae Leges* (25 January 1983).

John Paul II, Post-Synodal Apostolic Exhortation, *Pastoris Gregis* (2003).

Jones, E. Michael, *Living Machines: Bauhaus Architecture as Sexual Ideology* (San Francisco: Ignatius, 1995).

Kasper, Walter, 'Ecclésiologie eucharistique: de Vatican II à l'exhortation Sacramentum Caritatis', in L'Eucharistie, don de Dieu pour la vie du monde. Actes du Symposium international de théologie (Ottawa: CECC, 2009).

Kasper, Walter, 'The Theological Anthropology of *Gaudium et spes*', *Communio: International Catholic Review* 23 (1996), pp. 129–40.

Keenan, Marie, *Child Sexual Abuse and the Catholic Church: Gender, Power, and Organizational Culture* (Oxford: Oxford University Press, 2011).

Kerr, Fergus, *Twentieth-Century Catholic Theologians* (Oxford: Blackwell, 2006).

Kohak, Erazim, *The Embers and the Stars: A Philosophical Inquiry into the Moral Sense of Nature* (Chicago: University of Chicago, 1984).

Komonchak, Joseph, 'Toward an Ecclesiology of Communion', in Giuseppe Alberigo (ed.), *History of Vatican II* (English edn, ed. Joseph A. Komonchak; vol. 4; Maryknoll, NY: Orbis; Leuven: Peeters, 2003).

Lakeland, Paul, *Catholicism at the Crossroads: How the Laity Can Save the Church* (New York: Continuum, 2007).

Lamberts, Jozef, 'L'évolution de la notion de "participation active" dans le Mouvement liturgique du Vingtième siècle', *La Maison-Dieu* 241 (2005), pp. 77–120.

Läpple, Alfred, 'Interview by Gianni Valente and Pierlucca Azzardo', *30 Days* 1 (2006), pp. 54–60.

Larkin, Philip, 'Annus Mirabilis' in *High Windows* (London: Faber & Faber, 1974).

Legrand, Hervé, 'Communion eucharistique et communion ecclésiale. Une relecture de la première lettre aux Corinthiens', *Centro Pro Unione Bulletin* 67 (Spring 2005), pp. 21–32

Léon-Dufour, Xavier, 'Corps du Christ et Eucharistie selon saint Paul', in *Le corps et le corps du Christ dans la première Épître aux Corinthiens* (*Congrès de l'ACFEB, Tarbes,1981*) (Paris: Cerf, 1983).

Lonergan S. J., Bernard, *Method in Theology* (London: DLT, 1972).

Lonergan S. J., Bernard, 'The Response of the Jesuit, as Priest and Apostle, in the Modern World', in *Studies in the Spirituality of Jesuits* (1970).

McAuley, James, *The End of Modernity: Essays on Literature, Art and Culture* (Sydney: Angus and Robertson, 1959).

MacIntyre, Alasdair, *After Virtue: A Study in Moral Theory* (London: Duckworth, 1981).

Magister, Sandro, 'The impossible "Road Map of Peace with the Lefebvrists"' (9 February 2013), www.chiesa.espressonline.it.

Marcuse, Herbert, *One Dimensional Man* (Boston: Beacon Press, 1964).

Monge, Manuel Sánchez, *Eclesiología: La iglesia, misterio de comunión y misión* (Madrid: Sociedad de educación Atenas, 1994).

Montag, John, 'Revelation: The False Legacy of Suárez', in John Milbank (ed.), *Radical Orthodoxy* (London: Routledge, 1999).

Mora, Juan Manuel, *The Catholic Church, Opus Dei and the Da Vinci Code: A Global Communications Case Study* (Rome: Pontifical University of the Holy Cross, 2011).

Mühlen, Heribert, *L'Esprit dans l'Église: Una Mystica persona* (Paris: Cerf, 1969).

Murphy, Jeffrey J., 'The Lost (and Last) Animadversions of Daniel Mannix', *Australasian Catholic Record* 76 (1999), pp. 54–73.

Newman, John Henry, *An Essay on the Development of Christian Doctrine*, Sixth edn (South Bend: University of Notre Dame Press, 1989).

Newman, John Henry, 'Letter to the Duke of Norfolk', in *The Genius of John Henry Newman: Selections from his Writings* (Oxford: Clarendon Press, 1989).

Newman, John Henry Cardinal, Editorial in *The Rambler*, May 1859, quoted in 'Introduction', in *On Consulting the Faithful in Matters of Doctrine*, ed. with an introduction by John Coulson (London: Geoffrey Chapman, 1961).

O'Collins S. J., Gerald, 'Does Vatican II Represent Continuity or Discontinuity?' *Theological Studies* 74.1 (2012), pp. 768–94.

O'Donovan, Oliver, *A Conversation Waiting to Begin: The Churches and the Gay Controversy* (London: SCM Press, 2009).

O'Malley, John, *Tradition and Transition: Historical Perspectives on Vatican II* (Wilmington: M. Glazier, 1989).

O'Malley, John, *What Happened at Vatican II* (Cambridge, MA: Belknap of Harvard, 2008).

O'Meara, Thomas F., *A Theologian's Journey* (Boston: Paulist Press, 2002).

Ormerod, Neil, Ormond Rush, David Pascoe, Clare Johnson, and Joel Hodge (eds), *Vatican II: Reception and Implementation in the Australian Church* (Mulgrave, Vic: Garrett Publishing, 2013).

Orsy, Ladislas, *Receiving the Council: Theological and Canonical Insights and Debates* (Collegeville, MN: Liturgical, 2009).

Ouellet, Marc, *Divine Likeness: Toward a Trinitarian Anthropology of the Family* (Grand Rapids: Eerdmans, 2006).

Paul VI, General Audience Address of 26 November 1969.

Paul VI, Homily at the Mass in celebration of the IX anniversary of his papal coronation (29 June 1972).

Paul VI, *Presbyterorum Ordinis* (7 December 1965).

Paul VI, *Sacrosanctum Concilium* (4 December 1963).

Piacenza, Mauro Cardinal, Intervento del cardinal Mauro Piacenza, Perfetto della Congregazione per il Clero, Martedi, 4 ottobre, Los Angeles, Incontro con i Seminaristi. Text available in Italian at: www.clerus.org/clerus/dati/2011-09.

Pius X, Encyclical, *Vehementer Nos* (1906).

Pius XI, Letter to Cardinal Bertam, 13 November 1928, in Odile M. Liebard (ed.), *Clergy and Laity: Official Catholic Teachings* (Wilmington: McGrath, 1978).

Pottmeyer, Hermann, 'A New Phase in the Reception of Vatican II: Twenty Years of Interpretation of the Council', in Giuseppe Alberigo, Jean-Pierre Jossua, and Joseph A. Komonchak (eds.), *The Reception of Vatican II* (trans. Matthew J. O'Connell; Tunbridge Wells: Burns & Oats, 1987), pp. 27–43.

Rahner S. J., Karl, 'Notes on the Lay Apostolate', *Theological Investigations* (trans. Kark-H. Kruger; vol. 2; London: Darton, Longman and Todd, 1963).

Rahner S. J., Karl, 'Towards a Fundamental Interpretation of Vatican II', *Theological Studies* 40 (1979), pp. 716–27.

Ratzinger, Georg, *My Brother The Pope* [Original: *Mein Bruder, der Papst*] (trans. Michael J. Miller; San Francisco: Ignatius Press, 2011).

Ratzinger, Joseph, 'The Dignity of the Human Person', in Herbert Vorgrimler (ed.), *Commentary on the Documents of the Second Vatican Council* (London: Burns and Oates, 1969).

Ratzinger, Joseph, 'The Ecclesiology of the Constitution of the Church, Vatican II, *Lumen Gentium*,' November 2000, http://www.ewtn.com/library/CURIA/ CDFECCL.HTM. English trans. from *L'Osservatore Romano,* Weekly Edition in English, 19 September 2001.

Ratzinger, Joseph, *Theological Highlights of Vatican II* (New York: Paulist, 2009).

Romano, Claude, *L'événement et le monde.* Essais Philosophiques (Paris: Presses Universitaires de France, 1998).

Rush, Ormond, 'The Offices of Christ, *Lumen Gentium* and the People's Sense of the Faith', *Pacifica* 16 (2003), pp. 137–52.

Rush, Ormond, 'Toward a Comprehensive Interpretation of the Council and Its Documents', *Theological Studies* 73.3 (2012), pp. 547–69.

Sauer, Hanjo, 'The Council Discovers the Laity,' in Giuseppe Alberigo (ed.), *History of Vatican II* (vol. 4; Maryknoll, NY: Orbis, 2003), pp. 234–69.

Schillebeeckx OP, Edward, 'A New Type of Layman', in *The Mission of the Church* (trans. N. D. Smith; New York: Seabury, 1973).

Schillebeeckx OP, Edward, *Christ the Sacrament of the Encounter with God* (USA: Sheed & Ward, 1987).

Schindler, David L., 'Towards a Eucharistic Evangelisation', *Communio: International Catholic Review* 19 (Winter 1992), pp. 549–75.

Schmitz, Kenneth L., 'Postmodernism and the Catholic Tradition', *American Catholic Philosophical Quarterly* LXXIII.2 (1999), pp. 233–52.

Seasoltz, R. Kevin, 'Clericalism: A Sickness in the Church', *The Furrow: A Journal for the Contemporary Church* 61 (2010), pp. 135–42.

Second General Assembly, Extraordinary Synod of Bishops, *Ecclesia sub Verbo Dei Mysteria Christi Celebrans pro Salute Mundi. Relatio Finalis*, 1985.

Semmelroth, Otto, *Die Kirche als Ursakrament* (Frankfurt, a. M.: Knecht, 1955).

Suenens, Léon Cardinal, *Coresponsibility in the Church* (New York: Herder and Herder, 1968).

Suenens, Léon Cardinal, 'The Charismatic Dimension of the Church', in Yves Congar, Hans Küng, and Daniel O'Hanlon (eds.), *Council Speeches of Vatican II* (London and New York: Sheed and Ward, 1964).

Sullivan, Francis A., 'The Sense of Faith: The Sense/Consensus of the Faithful', in Bernard Hoose (ed.), *Authority in the Roman Catholic Church: Theory and Practice* (Aldershot, Hants: Ashgate, 2002).

Tertullian, *Apology* (ed. Carol Harrison; trans. Geoffrey D. Dunn; London: Routledge, 2004).

Theobald, Christoph, 'The Theological Options of Vatican II', in Alberto Melloni and Christoph Theobald (eds.), *Vatican II: A Forgotten Future* (London: SCM 2005).

Thérèse of Liseux, Lettre A, Soeur Marie du Sacré Coeur, Manuscrit (B 2v, 28) in *Sainte Thérèse de l'Enfant-Jésus et de la Sainte-Face: Oeuvres Complètes* (Paris: Cerf-Desclée de Brouwer, 1992).

Thomas Aquinas, *Summa theologiae*, IIIᵃ pars, q. 48, a. 2, ad 1.

Tillard, Jean-Marie Roger, *Église d'Églises. L'ecclésiologie de communion* (Paris: Cerf, 1987).

Trower, Philip, *Turmoil and Truth: The Historical Roots of the Modern Crisis in the Catholic Church* (San Francisco: Ignatius, 2003).

Valero, Jack and Austen Ivereigh, *Who Know Where They Stand: Catholic Voices and the Papal Visit to the UK* (Rome: Pontifical University of the Holy Cross, 2011).

Vatican Council II, *Christus Dominus*: Decree Concerning the Pastoral Office of Bishops (1965).

Vorgrimler, H. (ed.), *Commentary on the Documents of Vatican II* (5 vols; New York: Herder and Herder, 1967–69).

Wang, Stephen, *The New Evangelisation: What it is and how to do it* (Catholic Truth Society, London, 2013).

Weigel, George, *Evangelical Catholicism: Deep Reform in the 21st-Century Church* (Civitas Books, 2013).

Williams, Rowan, *Faith in the Public Square* (London: Bloomsbury, 2012).

Woodhead, Lisa, *The Westminster Faith Debates 2013: Religion in Personal Life*, http://faithdebates.org.uk/wp-content/uploads/2013/09/1368520681_Summary_Press_Releases_WFD2.pdf.

Zizioulas, Jean, *L'être ecclésial* (Geneva: Labor et Fides, 1981).

Zverina, Jozef, in Rudolf Battek, 'Spiritual values, independent initiatives and politics', in John Keane (ed.), *The Power of the Powerless* (London: Hutchinson, 1985).

CPSIA information can be obtained
at www.ICGtesting.com
Printed in the USA
LVHW052358081019
633575LV00005B/200/P